Praise for Pershey

"Pershey writes beautifully about hard things. This is not so much a book about ministry as it is about life. Pershey examines her motherhood, her marriage and her ministry as they are all unfolding, in their tender beginnings, all three, works in progress. Despite being a memoir of faith, this honest book is a sanctimony-free zone."

> —Lillian Daniel, pastor and coauthor of *This Odd and Wondrous Calling*

"In *Any Day A Beautiful Change,* Pershey shows us with candor and grace how motherhood, the chaos and delights of family, marriage, and our bodies enrich our interpretations of ministry, scripture and liturgy. I'm especially grateful for this memoir as a woman who has experienced pregnancy in the pulpit, but it is a gift for anyone who longs to reflect deeply on life and the church. It's funny and honest and wise."

> —Debbie Blue, pastor and author of *Sensual Orthodoxy*

D1113998

Any Day a Beautiful Change

A Story of Faith and Family

Katherine Willis Pershey

Any Day a Beautiful Change

A Story of Faith and Family

Katherine Willis Pershey

CHALICE
PRESS

ST. LOUIS, MISSOURI

Bible quotations, unless otherwise noted, are from the *New Revised Standard Version Bible*, copyright 1989, Division of Christian Education of the National Council of the Churches of Christ in the United States of America. Used by permission. All rights reserved.

Beautiful Change © 2003 The Innocence Mission, Badman Records. All rights reserved. Used by permission.

Goodbye California © 2011 Ram Island Songs, Box Tree Music. All rights on behalf of Songs Music Publishing o/b/o Ram Island Songs (ASCAP), Box Tree Music (ASCAP). All rights reserved. Used by permission.

Cover image: Photo copyright © 2012 by Marie Taylor of Marie Taylor photography (www.marietaylorphotography.com).

Cover design: Scribe Inc.

Cover design consultant: Elizabeth Dillow

www.chalicepress.com

PRINT: 9780827200296   EPUB: 9780827200302   EPDF: 9780827200319

**Library of Congress Cataloging-in-Publication Data
is available from the Library of Congress.**

For Ben, who said, "*You should write about us.*"

For Juliette: "*I'm writing this in part to tell you that if you ever wonder what you've done in your life, and everyone does wonder sooner or later, you have been God's grace to me, a miracle, something more than a miracle.*"

—MARILYNNE ROBINSON, *GILEAD*

And for Genevieve, who would not be if this had not been, and who is also pure grace and miracle.

Contents

Introduction

Juliette just had a temper tantrum. This morning I let her watch a shamefully long string of PBS Kids shows, far past the point where my guilt alarms start sounding. I told myself she needed the rest; for four days we've been sequestered in the house with influenza. I also needed the time. In a little over a week—just days after Juliette's third birthday—this manuscript I've been working on for much of her life is due to the publisher.

She didn't fuss because I turned off the television—even she knew that she had reached her limit. She fussed because she wanted me to play with her *right now*; I wanted to finish working on the paragraph I was revising. I bought myself a few more minutes by promising a round of Ants in the Pants if she would go fetch the game and set it up. She returned from her bedroom with the game in one hand and her hand-me-down tutu in the other. I helped her pull it on over her pajamas, hoping that an impromptu dance session would buy me even more time. But almost-three-year-olds don't only wear tutus to dance; they wear tutus for sick-day games of Ants in the Pants with their mamas, if only their mamas weren't so darn preoccupied writing books. I tried to buy one minute too many, and Juliette paid me back with a sorrowful fit. "I want you to play with me," she wailed.

I saved my document and drew my justifiably angry child onto my lap. "I know, honey, and I'm sorry," I whispered, pressing my cheek against her tear-streaked one. I picked up one of the books stacked on the bedside table: *The Middle Place*, by Kelly Corrigan, as beautiful, heartbreaking, and exquisite a book as ever could be. I ran my hand across the weathered cover, and considered the cover photograph of a little girl clad in yellow, suspended in air. Her expression is ambiguous; she could be midjump or midfall. "You know how I've told you that I'm writing a book?" I asked Juliette. She nodded. "It will be a book like this, a grown-up book with lots of words and no pictures, and my name will be on the front cover." She considered my words for a moment, in her quiet way, and traced a figure eight around the girl with her index finger. I knew that she understood, at least enough for the moment. I also knew precisely what she would say next: "Can we play *now*?"

I had just wanted a bound paperback, one whose pages would exhale that familiar papery breath when I skimmed them with my thumb. That the book I grabbed happened to be a mother's story was a coincidence. My bedside book stack is tall and its contents diverse; I could have just as easily selected *Heidi* or *A Heartbreaking Work of Staggering Genius* or *The Message*. Still, as I undertook the nearly impossible task of flipping plastic ants into an oddly eager dog's overalls, my mind wandered and I considered the similarity—and the dissimilarity—between that book and the one you hold in your hand (or, as the case may be, in your handheld device). Kelly Corrigan's younger daughters were just younger and just older than Juliette during the span of time *The Middle Place* captures. But what might have otherwise been a straightforward "mama memoir"—if there is such a thing—was transmuted by the same cells that mutated and multiplied within Corrigan's body. Her experience of early motherhood emerges from a wholly unexpected and harrowing context: her father's and her own concurrent encounters with cancer.

There but for the grace of God go I, I thought, even as I squirmed at the theologically untenable implications of this involuntary yet practically universal response to others' tribulations.

But my own experience of early motherhood had its own context, one that was not entirely unexpected. One that was, if not harrowing, at the very least vexing. The thing we worried wouldn't survive was not one of us, but *us*. This book that might have otherwise been a straightforward "mama memoir"—*there is no such thing*—became something else: a story of a marriage that could have but did not end only months after the birth of our daughter. I am proud of my daughter, excessively and unfashionably proud of my daughter. I just told Benjamin that Juliette Louise Pershey might be the best person I've ever met. But I am prouder still of the divorce we didn't seek, the marriage we stubbornly refused to forsake. We clutch it tenderly, especially in the moments in which it's still hard to discern if we are midjump or midfall, because it is the gift we are determined to give our family. Marriage is the boundary we established for the living of our lives, the context we have staked out for the story of our parenthood. In sickness and health and despair and joy, we belong to one another.

The story is complicated by another factor: Juliette is a preacher's kid, and Benjamin is a preacher's husband. Though once, early in my tenure as the first female solo minister of South Bay Christian Church, a member accidentally introduced Benjamin as the "pastor's wife." She turned crimson and smacked her hand over her mouth as soon as the phrase slipped off her tongue. (Fortunately, Benjamin laughed it off. If he hadn't, she might have actually died from embarrassment.) The concept of a pastor's husband is as novel as a female pastor, though increasingly less within the walls of mainline Christian denominations, which have been ordaining women for years. The thing is, more and more of the world exists beyond the walls of mainline Christian denominations, institutions that have wept and waved as their heyday departed. At beauty salons and train stations, on daytime television and in Roman Catholic parishes, most everyone expects ministers to be men. I met a new friend—now a much beloved friend—when I was pregnant. We'd first connected online; I loved the songs Allison posted on MySpace, and after I wrote her a dopey fan letter, she looked up my church website and read a handful of archived sermons before writing a (markedly less dopey) fan letter in return. When we met for lunch at a Marina del Rey *crêperie*, we discussed the social networking site that had brought us together. Everyone loved to hate MySpace, though the free publicity was a boon for musicians like Allison. "But it's the people that it's brought into my life that I love the most," she gushed. Allison *loves* people. "Some of the wildest characters!" I was curious, and said so. Thus far, MySpace had brought Allison into my life, and she wasn't an especially wild character. She got a funny look on her face, a look I couldn't quite read, and gently said, "*You* are a wild character, Katherine. You're a *pregnant pastor*."

I hadn't thought of it that way. But I was a pregnant pastor, and soon after a pastor who was also the mama of a nursing infant.

I'm not entirely sure how being a pastor colors my mothering. I'm sure I would be a different mother if I were a lawyer or pharmaceutical saleswoman, but that's an irrelevant tautology. I would also be a different person. I do know that there are aspects of pastoral ministry that have made parenting a young child significantly easier. The church is a built-in community. The apostle Paul borrowed familiar language to describe the unique relationship between Christians, calling us brothers and sisters in Christ. In both of the congregations I have served, my daughter has benefited from a seemingly endless supply of brothers and sisters in Christ—as well as aunts and uncles and grandmas and grandpas in Christ. That isn't proprietary to her as a preacher's kid; anyone who joins a tight-knit community of faith is adopted into the family, though the children of preachers may be woven more tightly than most into that shared fabric.

The flexibility I've been afforded, first as a solo minister of a tiny congregation, and more unusually as an associate minister of a large church, is a godsend. Although I have worked full time since Juliette was five weeks old, I've never completely resonated with the classic image of the working mother, dashing out the door in the morning only to return, spent, at the end of the day. Days like that have been few and far between. I often come home for lunch and decide to work from home for the rest of the day. Juliette routinely spends a couple of hours in my private church study, a luxury we wouldn't have if I inhabited a cubicle from nine to five. When she was a baby, I often propped her on my hip after the worship service; she helped me greet the church members as they filed through the stained glass doors. On a few occasions, when it seemed appropriate, I brought her along when I visited church members at their homes. Some of my colleagues condemn this practice, believing that the pastoral visit is solely a time for spiritual care. All I know is the look of pure delight those lonely shut-ins flashed when I came accompanied by a chubby, slobbery, giggly baby; providing a dose of delight is surely a variation of spiritual care. They only let us leave after I promised to bring her back. Such a permeable line between work and family is rare, if not unique to ministry.

My vocation as a parish pastor certainly shapes this story. There are parts of the story I simply cannot tell because they are not mine to tell. Ministers help bear the burdens of others, and more often than not, we bear those burdens confidentially. I claim no right to divulge the private joys and sorrows of those in my care, not even when those joys and sorrows affected me enough to affect my family's life. I am comfortable with the handful of lacunas in this book, the places where only I could know that a few pages are missing. I am significantly less comfortable with the places where I wish I could scrap the truth for happier (albeit fictitious) versions of my family and myself. Everyone knows—or should by now—that pastors aren't perfect. I don't feel a responsibility to live up to an impossible ideal. Still, as a pastor, I guard my own private joys and sorrows fairly closely. I don't believe it is the duty of my church to bear my burdens, at least not in the same way I bear theirs. That isn't to say they shouldn't care for me—and oh, have they cared for me. We have consumed a great deal of homemade soup in our day, most of it made in the homes of my parishioners. But I keep my crises at an arm's length from my church, or at least try.

Though it happens from time to time, as a writer I try to refrain from "bleeding on the page." Much in the same way I try to refrain from crying at church, though that happens, too. Once, when I'd just learned our dog, Deacon, had developed terminal lymphoma, I decided not to mention it during the time in worship when members shared prayer requests. Not because a sick dog was unworthy of their prayers; they were a generous crowd who would pray about any little thing that troubled your heart. I didn't share the news because I knew I would fall apart if I did. But one animal lover knew of Deacon's prognosis and took it upon herself—completely innocuously—to announce it to the congregation. As soon as she began speaking I crumpled into the front pew and wept, frantically trying to regain enough composure to go on with the show. Complicating my sadness was a newfound panic that my church could no longer trust me to be their pastor—if I emotionally unraveled over a sick pit bull, how could I ever provide pastoral care to a human being with a terminal illness? I didn't even feel like a pastor. I felt like a little girl.

There are things in this story that make me feel like a little girl, that make my cheeks burn with embarrassment, that I have struggled to share with close friends and family. These are things I have never uttered before a congregation during the time of joys and concerns. And yet, here is a book about me—about my experience of motherhood, marriage, and ministry during a season of profound joys and sorrows—bound and ready to whisper my secrets at the turn of a page.

Will they still let me be their pastor?

It's a chance I'm willing to take. There is something to be said for authenticity, let alone the indwelling presence of the Holy Spirit. Ultimately, I am not merely telling my story. I am participating in the timeworn tradition of testimony, pointing to God's work in the world, starting with God's work in my life. It is my prayer that the people I serve will not begrudge my need for grace, especially because I have been preaching all along that it is grace by which we all are saved. (It can't hurt that the senior pastor in my new congregation grew up in the church; I've lost count of how many people have stopped in the hall to tell me the story of how, as a boy, he escaped Sunday school by climbing out of a window. These are folks who understand that ministers are ordinary people.)

I didn't yet know if the story would end happily when I began telling it, but I staked my hopes in a vision borrowed from a favorite song lyric by The Innocence Mission: "At any time I could change, any day, a beautiful change." Mine is a story of beautiful changes: the birth of a daughter, the healing of a marriage, the closing of one good ministry and the start of another, committed to paper even as they were yet unfolding, between temper tantrums and arguments and committee meetings and lazy Saturday mornings spent at the ocean, watching schools of dolphins feeding in the Santa Monica Bay. Any day, a beautiful change.

It has been so, and by the grace of God, may it continue to be.

1

Before

Before my life was braided into a pattern shaped by marriage, ministry, and motherhood, I spent many a Friday night perched in the smoky loft of Brady's Cafe in Kent, Ohio. It has since been subsumed by Starbucks, and while I have yet to bring myself to return, I imagine that its quirky charm has been scrubbed clean. The new corporate management surely doesn't let graffiti flourish in the ladies' room or toss locally grown nasturtiums into the early summer salads, and the poets didn't even bother to ask if they could keep holding their monthly open poetry readings on the premises.

The place closed down the same weekend my husband and I left for California; we missed the going-out-of-business extravaganza— part celebration, part wake, part auction. My parents stopped in long enough to bid on one of the blue glass vases that used to hold sunflowers in the windowsill overlooking Main Street as a going-away present. We'd both been regulars, especially at the poetry nights. We met in a creative writing class when I was a sophomore. Benjamin was older by five years, and though he'd come to Kent State as a student, he was really more of a townie by that point. He didn't live in a dorm, or even one of the countless shabby student rentals. He lived in a halfway house for recovering alcoholics. I knew this because of the poems he read in class and at the coffeehouse. I'd never met anyone so shy yet so willing to tell unflattering truths about himself. It was as though he'd discovered that the truth was air; if he wasn't honest he would die, or at the very least start drinking again. Sometimes, when it was his turn at the microphone at Brady's, he walked up empty-handed and composed poems on the spot. To me, it was even more inexplicable than those monks who sweep their intricate mandalas into piles of sand. Each line only existed in the moment it was being uttered. The community that gathered around cigarettes and coffee cups and words at Brady's Cafe loved to mythologize its members, and Benjamin was an epic character.

That said, while I started paying attention to Benjamin the moment I met him, I was too busy being nineteen to pay *too* much attention. I was equally into boys and religion—one particular boy, and increasingly, one particular religion. I came out as a Christian in our poetry class, reading a poem in which I imagined myself sharing a beer with Jesus. It was a decent poem, decent enough to win me a cash prize in the annual undergraduate writing contest and make me think I was *all that*. The truth was that I'd written it because my boyfriend had praised another girl's Jesus poem. Within the year, the boyfriend ditched me. Not only was I devastated in the way you can only be when you've meticulously renovated your whole personality to make someone love you, but I wasn't even sure I wanted to have anything to do with the faith I'd hastily adopted to please him. Not that Christianity was new to me; I was baptized as an infant on Palm Sunday with water from the Jordan River. Since high school, I'd tinkered with the idea of becoming a minister. I'd had a vision, an ordinary one without any bells or whistles or burning bushes. I simply could see myself standing in the pulpit of a church. Yet I had a minor issue: I wasn't entirely sure I believed in God. It struck me that this particular qualification was every bit as crucial as, say, perfect vision is for fighter pilots. Before the born-again boyfriend came along, I'd been exploring the Unitarian Universalist tradition, in which one can feasibly be a minister without sporting orthodox ideas about the divine.

So began a new epoch of my young life, an epoch mottled with heartbreak, anger, confusion, regret, and an embarrassing degree of dumb flailing as I strived to find substitutes to fill the gaping holes in my heart. Ever the poet, I committed it all to notebook paper. I cringe to recall how many such pages I forced upon my friends at the coffeehouse. (One of the things I hadn't lost in my grand devastation was the belief that, so far as poetry went, I was still *all that*.) If I had enough of an impression on the crowd to earn myself a mythology,

I don't want to know what it was. In the meantime, I decided to accept the position I'd been offered just before things started falling apart. Therefore I started my first church job—as a youth ministry director—a closet agnostic on the rebound in more ways than one.

I was a wreck.

I was a peculiar wreck; by contemporary standards of collegiate behavior, I was quite tame. I simply couldn't bear to be alone, and thus threw myself into a series of increasingly ill-advised flings, each consciously designed to make me forget that I had voluntarily obliterated myself for someone who didn't love me anymore. I succeeded only in making myself feel worse. Worst of all, I began to suspect that I was disappointing God. Surely, even the beer-buzzed Jesus I'd conjured for my poem wouldn't approve of such an ineffective and superficial healing technique. I didn't know how to extract myself from my own wreckage, so I tried the next best thing: I fled the country.

Responsibly, of course, I fled through a university-sanctioned study abroad program. I may have been an emotional spastic (my sincere apologies to the boys I dated in that era, especially the nice one), but even I couldn't let my broken heart or my spiritual crisis get in the way of my intention to graduate in four years, preferably with honors. Unsurprisingly, I lugged all of my issues with me to Mexico. My journal, which one of these days I shall burn with great satisfaction, testifies against me. But then midway through the summer, just shy of my twenty-first birthday, I received a letter from Benjamin. Three pages, one-sided, printed on the cheap yellow stationery my mother used to pick up at the dime store. He asked me out in the last line.

I'd hoped—even expected—to hear from him. I hadn't seen him much since our poetry class ended, but in the spring, we had reconnected at a festival honoring the poet James Wright. I'd carpooled down to southern Ohio with friends, and when we pulled up to the Knight's Inn Motel, he was leaning against his door, smoking a cigarette. He'd come alone; we were all surprised and happy to see him. That night our friends drank, and they were too tired to wake up for the morning readings. Benjamin drove me to the festival in his pickup truck. At lunchtime, our friends still hadn't reappeared, so Benjamin and I took a table for two at a diner in downtown Martins Ferry. It was the first time we talked about anything other than poetry. Indeed, he was such a quiet guy that I hadn't heard him talk much at all, except to read his poems. I was surprised that there was more to him than the wounded intensity he funneled into his writing. He bragged about his brilliant niece and told funny stories about Laverne and Raymond, his grandparents. Most of all, though, he listened. I could even see him doing it. Due to poor hearing in his left ear, he cocked his head at an angle to catch my words before they were lost in the noisy restaurant. At the end of the day, I made up an excuse to catch a ride back to Kent in his pickup and offered to buy him a chocolate milkshake in return. When he dropped me off, though, I dashed out of the car, not giving him enough time to ask for my telephone number. I still maintain that the primary reason was that I really had to pee. I did. But I also was afraid, though not of getting involved with an alcoholic. If anything, his candidness about his problem and his desire to heal were appealing. What scared me was the prospect of involving myself—my wrecked self—with someone I might actually damage in my flailing. Reservations notwithstanding, I'd made sure he received a copy of my summer address.

Even more than the shy invitation to go out for dinner upon my return, another sentence caught me: *I hope there are things you won't even know how to write about.* I was startled by how fervently I hoped Benjamin would be one of those things, and I knew that if I dared fall in love with him, it had better be for good.

I wrote back to accept the dinner date. We married on my twenty-second birthday.

Our courtship was quick in part because I'd returned from my summer abroad with the intention to attend seminary as soon as I graduated from Kent State University. At the time I thought my faith was as shaky as ever, but in retrospect the leaps of faith I was taking were big enough to be downright foolhardy. We jumped into our marriage as if we were being chased by a shotgun, but it wasn't an unplanned pregnancy but our mutual need that yoked us. We needed each other almost as much as we loved each other. The whole thing could have gone either way, and if we really mean to be honest— Benjamin still treats honesty as if it were as precious as oxygen, and

I've learned to as well—we always knew ours was a risky union. But it's a risk I would never take back, not even during our worst moments (or years, for that matter: year one and year six).

Some Christian traditions classify marriage as an official sacrament: a means of grace. Keep in mind that baptism is also a sacrament, and though on the surface it appears the one being baptized is merely getting wet, the descent into the waters signifies death to self. That's mighty fierce grace; some of us need such fierceness, like Benjamin, and me. Through our marriage, we have learned that there is a difference between coming of age and growing up, a difference as broad as the chasm between not drinking and true sobriety. We have worked terrifically hard, not to earn grace (grace can never be earned) but to honor the grace we are so freely given.

Another gracious gift I have received is gentler, all things considered. As it turned out, I took to ministry as if it were what I was supposed to do all along. I'm fairly sure it is. I thought I was too broken and confused to be of use to God or the church, but that isn't the way it works. It's amazing that the gospel gets so twisted. Jesus' words are unambiguous: "I have come to call not the righteous but sinners" (Mk. 2:17). My work as a pastor has brought me such great joy I can't bear to imagine how my life would have unfolded if I hadn't barreled into seminary as blindly as we charged into our marriage. I wouldn't feel the weight of a dying woman's hand, clasping mine for a prayer. I wouldn't experience the thrill of playing with biblical texts in the pulpit week after week. I wouldn't know the comfort of completely fitting in when I gather with other clergy. It isn't all Easter lilies, but I swear: I even loved redrafting the bylaws that govern the church board.

What can I say? Sometimes youthful foolhardiness is rewarded. Greatly.

First comes love, then comes marriage, then comes the minister with a baby carriage.

2

Send the Love Inward

Poor Mary. I have such empathy for her plight. Not only do Christians eternally refer to her by the shorthand "virgin," reducing her personhood to the status of her sexual (in)activity, but she's also endured centuries of well-meaning reverence for her role in bearing the Christ child. Sure, everybody loves those four weeks of "spiritual" pregnancy in Advent, preparing the way for the baby Jesus to be born anew in our hearts each year. Mary knows best that the gestation of a savior takes a heck of a lot longer than four weeks. Assuming the Holy Spirit didn't give the sacred fetus a head start on development, Mary carried that child for roughly forty weeks. Theologians may wax poetic about the figurative loveliness of it all, but our exalted and exhausted virgin was too busy being literally pregnant. I wonder what got to her most—the incessant urination, morning sickness, swollen ankles, strangers stroking her bump? And then, the worst injustice of all: being forced to strike an eternally serene pose in innumerable Christmas crèches, as if labor pains were the real myth in this story. Paul, of all people, *Paul* was the one to get it right: there is a lot of groaning involved in birthing a new creation. And pain. And fear.

During my own literal (and nonvirginal) pregnancy, I did my fair share of groaning. And griping and freaking out and other such things that trespass against the way pregnant women are supposed to be. I approached the entirety of my pregnancy with a low-level panic. I had wanted to be pregnant . . . mostly. In truth, I had been so unsure about motherhood that I refused to admit that my husband and I were trying to conceive. I confessed to close friends that we "weren't preventing." After years of unsettled discernment, I had finally surrendered myself to the likelihood that I would never find clarity about whether or not I was called to become a mother. If Benjamin and I were going to have a baby, it was just going to happen.

And happen it did. After feeling miserable for a couple of weeks and realizing it might have been awhile since my last period, I bought a home pregnancy test. When the stick produced a faint pink cross, I giggled out loud. Like the biblical Sarah, who laughed when the angel predicted her elder-years pregnancy, my laugh revealed as much nervous disbelief as cautious delight. I practiced telling my husband in the bathroom mirror. "I'm pregnant" sounded self-centered; "We're having a baby," too presumptuous. Even though I wasn't yet over my mixed feelings about conceiving, I was already terrified about the possibility of miscarriage. I did a quick inventory of my recent activities—had I used bleach without proper ventilation? Taken too hot a shower? What about that sushi I had for lunch last week? In that first hour of knowing I was pregnant, I was introduced to the physical, emotional, and spiritual conditions that would be my constant companions for the next nine months: nausea, lethargy, guilt, fear, excitement, and perhaps a hint of something you could call joy. The zygote and my ambivalence would multiply at about the same rate.

Although my pregnancy was healthy and normal, the physical symptoms clobbered me. I wasn't bone tired; I was blood tired, as if exhaustion were a heavy fluid circulating through my whole body. I had always approached my work as a parish pastor with passion, focus, and energy, and suddenly I found myself sneaking home from church to collapse on the couch. During my first trimester, I got hooked on afternoon reruns of Scrubs. I'm fairly sure I watched every available episode of the series in those three months. Yet no amount of investment in the on-again, off-again romance between J. D. and Elliot made watching Scrubs part of my job description. Though I felt physically incapable of doing much more than the bare minimum, the guilt of being a lazy pastor gnawed at me (even as I gnawed on anything edible that crossed my path). My sister tried to convince me that women have had to half-ass their way through pregnancy since the dawn of time and civilization persists, but I couldn't shake the feeling that my pregnancy was causing me to betray my commitment to my congregation.

My pregnancy did alter my relationship with the church where I served as a solo pastor, though not in the manner I expected. As my waist went on sabbatical and my zippers were replaced by dowdy elastic, my parishioners were positively beside themselves with anticipation. If there was any ambivalence on their part that their pastor was pregnant, they didn't show it. They lavished us with prayer and presents. The attention was a little unnerving, to be honest. Here I felt like I was doing less for them, and here they were, loving me more than ever. It was almost as though my changing body were ministering to them of its own volition. The reason was clear: I was a walking—er, waddling—symbol of new life. My church, which had called me as a twenty-four-year-old straight out of seminary, was declining. The congregation was so small and graying it hadn't birthed any babies in fifteen years. After such a barren spell, to have a pregnant woman in their midst was tantamount to a revival. As much as I chuckled at the maternity shirt I saw a few years ago that was emblazoned with the words *Doing My Part for Church Growth*, that pressure adds rather a lot to your pregnancy weight. I didn't know if this new dimension to our relationship was healthy. The boundary training I received in seminary taught me that the body is suspect when it comes to ministry. Bodies have gotten a lot of pastors in trouble. The notion that my pregnant body was somehow ministering to my congregation independent of my reasoning faculties completely freaked me out. But just as there was no stopping my belly from growing, there was no harnessing my parishioners' response to it as a symbol of new life.

Because at the most basic level, that's precisely what a baby bump is, symbolically *and* literally. There is new life performing amniotic acrobatics in there. And when I was about six months along, I realized that the new life within me—which was so apparent to everyone around me—was not yet real to me. Like the cinematically knocked-up Juno, I too "heard in health class that pregnancy often results in an infant." Heck, I felt her digging her toes into my bladder at three in the morning. We had even learned she was a "she." But my reasoning faculties were once again failing to keep up with my experience of pregnancy. I knew there was a baby in my womb . . . but that knowledge was weirdly theoretical. There was none of that bonding illustrated on all the maternity books with soft-focus photographs of hugely pregnant women smiling and stroking their bumps—no real sense of relationship. I wouldn't say I didn't love her, if love, as the cliché imparts, is a verb. I did everything I was supposed to do to nurture her well-being, from taking my vitamins to sacrificing my beloved coffee to knitting a baby kimono in ivory kitchen cotton. But my few attempts at singing and talking to her were profoundly awkward; for while I may have felt her kicks, I didn't feel her *presence*. I may have known she was there, but I didn't know *her*. And that made me feel terribly ashamed. I was failing at something that came naturally to all the other mothers-to-be. The oddest thing was that the situation was vaguely familiar: a being so intimate as to be within me, yet my inability to relate to said being with anything other than theoretical acknowledgement and stock responses.

Oh my God.

No, not quite. More like: *O my God!*

I related to the fetus growing within me the same way I related to God. Or more accurately, I struggled to relate to the fetus growing within me the same way I have struggled to relate to God my entire life.

I believe in God. I believe in God enough to have discerned a call to ministry, enough to immerse myself in theological studies, enough to preach the good news Sunday after Sunday. But my belief in God has flourished almost entirely in my head. It's an intellectual belief that has rarely managed to navigate the short yet treacherous pathway between my head and my heart. To put it plainly, I have a hard time *feeling* God. Although I've endured bouts of what you might call classical doubt, the crux of my God problem truly isn't that I question God's existence. It's that my intellectual belief, bereft of lived experience, reduces God to a theoretical being. One that I know is there, but do not know. The awkwardness that caused me to trail off halfway through humming lullabies in the general direction of my uterus? Yeah, I know that feeling. It descends upon me when I try to pray. As if I am talking to an imaginary friend who is simultaneously the Creator of the universe. And despite reassurances to the contrary, I stubbornly insist that everyone else but me is vividly experiencing God.

As with my pregnancy, all the signs demonstrate the reality of this Life that is the Source of Life. When I sing the doxology each week in worship, praising God from whom all blessings flow, I mean it. Wherever love, justice, hope, and peace prevail, I see fingerprints of the divine. I'm even relatively sure I've been the recipient of spiritual kicks from God. I tearfully flung questions at a wise mentor: *How can a baby/God who is so intimate as to live within me somehow not be real to me? How can I not feel the presence of one/One who is in the process of radically transforming my life? How can I hold it together when I'm inundated with shame and inadequacy on top of all those crazy-making pregnancy hormones?* His advice was simple: relax and send the love inward. And of course that's the hardest thing to do. Sending the love inward meant having the courage and imagination to love the baby I hadn't yet met. Sending the love inward meant loving the God I hadn't yet seen. Sending the love inward even meant loving myself.

It would be so much easier to love her when I could just hold her, I told myself. I wouldn't struggle to know her when I could actually meditate on her impossibly tiny fingernails instead of just squint at the ghostly sonogram. When she became tangible enough to take into my arms, surely she would cease to be an intellectual theory with the uncanny power to make me pee. Yes, I told myself. Even if I can't turn this neurotic pregnancy around, when this being is made flesh, I will never doubt her again. I'll sing her lullabies until my throat gets hoarse. I'll love her so much it will saturate my heart and leak from my breasts.

(And here it is again.) Oh my God. *O my God!*

"And the Word became flesh and lived among us, and we have seen his glory, the glory as of a father's only son, full of grace and truth" (Jn. 1:14). Incarnation. God becomes flesh. God becomes a baby. The very fundamentals of my religious tradition, the stuff I'd grown up with and studied and (for heaven's sake!) *preached* was suddenly extraordinarily real to me. The longing I had for my theoretical fetus to be transformed into a tangible baby was the same as my desire for my theoretical divinity to become the incarnate Christ. I needed the inarguable reality of flesh and blood to anchor my motherhood and my faith.

I needed Jesus and Juliette.

You should have heard my Christmas Eve sermon. I was only eight months along, though from the look of me you'd have guessed I wouldn't make it through the last verse of *Silent Night*. I was done staving off the ridiculously rich symbolism of my body; that sermon nearly wrote itself. I cracked the obligatory jokes—"put me on a don-key right now, I'd go into labor, too." I connected the dots between liturgy and life:

> In the weeks before Christmas, we are called to wait and hope and prepare our hearts for the birth of the Christ child. For us, these spiritual attitudes have been accompanied by a whole host of practicalities as we prepare for the birth of the one who is presently hiding behind the pulpit. Folding the freshly laundered layette and building the crib were as much a part of our seasonal activities as lighting the candles of the Advent wreath.

I carefully extricated myself from the spotlight:

> My silent sidekick brings the focus of this holy night into unmistakable clarity: it's all about a baby. Not just any baby— though every baby is a blessed reminder of the one whom we gather to worship. This night is about a baby named Jesus.

And I brought it all home:

> Our Christmas work, our share of the holy child care, is to nurture and to love the new life that longs to be born in our hearts on this night. Like Mary, our work is just beginning, and will inevitably change us. There's no going back once we've worshiped at the manger.

There was no social commentary about how Jesus was born into poverty, no theological explication of the doctrine of the incarnation. A connoisseur of Christmas Eve sermons might have found it a tad pedestrian. But I felt the truth of it every bit as strongly as I believed the truth of it.

And then, one miserably pregnant month later, I went into labor and delivered the child. I was terrified. I, who prefer to live in my mind, was having such an intensely bodily experience I couldn't even remember how to think. But when I finally wasn't pregnant anymore, when I finally felt myself splitting open to make way for the very real, very tangible head of my daughter, everything went blurry but the face of Juliette. I not so much thought but felt: She is so familiar. I know her and love her. And I've known her and loved her all along. I'm not just called to be a mother. I'm called to be *her* mother. Thanks be to God.

3

Push Like You're Angry

I spent the first twenty minutes of my daughter's life getting stitches, well, *you know where.* One would think that a little needle and thread would be inconsequential compared to labor and delivery, or that I, as the beatific new mother, would be so overcome with hormones and adoration for my newborn that I wouldn't mind the person in a white coat playing seamstress with my ladyparts.

One would be wrong. Every prick of the needle was sharpened by my seething hatred of my obstetrician.

I had only been Dr. Hernandez's patient since I was thirty weeks into my pregnancy. The first practice from which I received prenatal care rankled me too much and too often. I saw a seemingly interchangeable muster of intervention-happy doctors and was convinced that if I stuck with them, I would end up scheduled for a cesarean, regardless of whether it was truly necessary. My last straw for that practice snapped when the obstetrician visibly rolled her eyes at me when I dared utter the phrase "birth plan."

Naomi Wolf's *Misconceptions* may not have been the most comforting book to read while pregnant, thick as it is with horrifying statistics, anecdotes, and observations about the highly medicalized, litigation-driven realm of contemporary obstetrics, but it did confer upon me the backbone to recognize and reject mediocre prenatal care. I jumped ship to an osteopath listed on my insurance company's preferred providers. During our first appointment, I communicated that I needed a doctor who listened to me and who was committed to helping me deliver my baby as safely and naturally as possible. She nodded and murmured sympathetically enough to convince me that she was the one.

The sign that she was not the one came a few appointments later, at thirty-nine weeks—a little too late in the game to be getting persnickety. It's impossible to explain the situation without talking even more about my soon-to-be-traumatized ladyparts, but let's face it: *childbearing generally involves vaginas.* Dr. Hernandez was poking around in my cervix in order to determine how dilated it was. Jackpot: a centimeter! Which meant I could go into labor in ten minutes or in two weeks (read: the latter). Satisfied with her find, she proceeded to ask me if I wanted her to strip my membranes.

Um, what now? Strip my membranes?

I swear I read all my pregnancy and childbirth books. I paid attention to the teacher in the Lamaze class we dutifully took at the hospital. I could have drawn a detailed diagram of an occupied uterus, so well versed in the stuff of babymaking was I. Yet I drew a complete blank at this mildly alarming phrase.

An exchange of questions and answers followed. Dr. Hernandez patiently reminded me that stripping membranes involves manually separating the amniotic sac from the inside of the cervix. No, it doesn't really hurt, but neither does it feel good. No, there's no promise that it will actually make you go into labor.

So, Dr. Hernandez, what would you use to strip my membranes? Oh? Your finger? How convenient, *since it's been tickling my cervix throughout this entire conversation.* (Note to obstetricians and gynecologists: please try to explain procedures to your patients before you are all up in their business.)

I tell two distinct versions of Juliette's birth. There's the chipper one I pull out for polite company. That one tarries at the desk of the emergency room, where Benjamin and I showed up at two in the morning. I hate being cold, so even when all the other Southern Californians were wearing light jackets, I often wore an oversized green parka for early morning walks with the dog and, in this instance, earlier morning trips to labor and delivery. My parka was so large I could zip it up around my pregnant lady girth (which, incidentally, makes me think maybe I should retire it for something a little more flattering).

That night my parka was zippered up to my chin. The man at the desk appraised us blankly. "My wife is having . . . um, contractions," Benjamin mumbled, not entirely at ease with his new role as the family spokesperson. I'm the one who usually informs the hostess how many will be joining our party for dinner and requests the check when we're finished. The receptionist's expression remained unchanged, not registering the information. All of a sudden I remembered that I was not obviously pregnant in my watermelon coat, so I gasped, "I'm in labor!"

As we trudged down the hallway in the prescribed direction, I commented that he couldn't discern my condition on account of my outerwear.

"Yeah, they thought someone from Alaska was injured," Benjamin wisecracked, successfully making me laugh through a beastly contraction. From there the story hits a few generic points. My cervix dilated three to seven centimeters in forty minutes. I reneged on my plan to say no to drugs; rather, I wanted to hug the anesthesiologist. Benjamin was phenomenal, and once I convinced my mother to stop wringing her hands and making inappropriately pained expressions during every contraction, she was great as well. According to Benjamin, Juliette popped out like a balloon in the Macy's Thanksgiving Day Parade.

Sometimes I let it slip that there were a few frightening and unpleasant moments, but I'm always quick to follow up with a reassurance. All in all it was a surreal, fascinating, amazing experience. Of course I bawled when I saw Juliette's little face.

The other version of the story drowns in that which was frightening and unpleasant. While my cervix dilated at the speed of light, the baby's heart rate dipped a hair, likely due to my panicky reaction to the pain. Nurses darted around the room, hooking me up to oxygen and injecting my arm with a drug to slow down the contractions. Benjamin held my hand and tried not to look as terrified as he felt. When Juliette is an obstinate teenager, I will try my best to be a good mother and not remind her that my water broke while I was throwing up on the delivery bed (*after all I've done for you, child . . .*). Sweet baby *Jesus*, did it hurt. But that nasty spell ended as quickly as it began. The epidural drugs kicked in and the pain eased to an occasional twinge. Never before and never since have I felt so mellow. Benjamin napped for an hour and I listened to music, completely oblivious to the contractions roiling my uterus. I remember being vaguely aware that I was going to have a baby within the next few hours, but I was too chilled out to get worked up about it.

It has dawned on me that maybe there was something else in the IV. I'll never know.

The nurse determined I was ready to push at seven in the morning. "I'll page your doctor to let her know your progress," she said, giving my foot an encouraging squeeze that I saw but did not feel. A few minutes later she returned looking bemused. "She wants you to wait another hour before you push."

OK, then. The hour passed quickly, part of it taken up with pushing lessons during which I wasn't actually allowed to push. My husband and mother were briefed on their roles; Benjamin would grip one of my legs, and my mother would help lift my shoulders as I curled into the pushes.

When we finally commenced, I discovered that pushing was kind of fun. I'm sure I wouldn't have experienced it the same way if I had been drenched in sweat and crawling up the walls from the torture of transition; the epidural had me covered. I was chatting and joking and drinking as much forbidden cranberry juice as I could slip behind the nurse's back. (Despite the fact that giving birth requires enormous physical effort, many hospitals do not allow women in labor to eat or drink, on account of the likelihood that one in three of them will end up in the operating room.)

Around a quarter to nine, the nurse informed me I had to stop pushing. "We shouldn't go any further without the doctor, but she's on her way," she said apologetically. I could tell she was ticked at the doctor. I certainly was. Not pushing was infinitely harder than pushing. The effect was something like trying not to pee, not to sneeze, not to cough, and not to orgasm—conflated into one uncontainable urge. After ten minutes of refraining, I burst into tears. Something had to be released. I was still crying when Dr. Hernandez finally showed. She glanced at me and turned to the nurse. "Is the epidural not working?"

A "hello" would have been nice. Perhaps even an "I'm so sorry that my inexcusable tardiness has been torturing you." Addressing the nurse as if I weren't even in the room: not so nice.

Within minutes, Dr. Hernandez talked me into getting the episiotomy I so dreaded. With the snip of her scissors, the last of my illusions about an intervention-free childbirth dissolved.

The pushing blessedly recommenced. With Dr. Hernandez in the room and the crowning imminent, the atmosphere intensified. "Push harder!" she barked. Benjamin and my mother chimed in, rooting me on. The music player, which had been playing calming folksongs, shuffled in a Christina Aguilera song I'd thrown onto the labor list on a whim.

How I wish I could have channeled any one of the stereotypically bitchy women giving birth that inhabit so many movie scenes. I desperately wanted everyone, Christina included, to *shut the hell up*. But I'm a good girl. I didn't want to be rude to my (rude) doctor, let alone my husband and my mama, who clearly meant well even if the penultimate moments of my labor inspired them to impersonate Will Ferrell and Cheri Oteri playing spastic Spartan cheerleaders on Saturday Night Live.

I took a deep breath and, along with my next push, let out the biggest "shush" noise I've ever created in my life. Of course, nobody got it that I was actually trying to communicate. They just thought I forgot to hold my breath the way I was supposed to.

That's when Dr. Hernandez barked the directive that burned itself into my brain and played on repeat for months: "Push like you're angry."

Push like you're angry.

Had I not been otherwise occupied having a baby, I would have explained to Dr. Hernandez that her approach was neither helpful nor appropriate. Tell me to push like I'm joyful. Tell me to push like I'm powerful. Tell me to push like I'm about to meet my daughter. Don't tell me to push like I'm *angry*.

Even as a whole part of me was opening up to make way for the child, another part of me was shutting down. In a moment in which I should have felt invincible, I was rendered powerless. I just had to get through it. What infuriates me the most is that I did push like I was angry, because I was angry.

The rush of seeing Juliette for the first time supplanted my rage, but when she was whisked away to be weighed and I was left with Dr. Hernandez and her needle, it returned to a simmer. I would learn soon enough that Dr. Hernandez was a particularly poor ladyparts seamstress, and that my wound wouldn't heal properly.

My anger boiled.

I know that hormones are potent. The lingering baby blues colored my perception, for sure. When I was telling this story to a friend, I got to the part about Dr. Hernandez's egregious delivery room utterance, fully expecting that she would react with shock and indignance. But there was this pause—infinitesimal but long for me to detect that the shock and indignation that followed did so only because I nonverbally cued it: *you're supposed to think this is the worst thing you've ever heard.* The fact is that Dr. Hernandez presided over a birth that was essentially uncomplicated, for mother and for baby. Of course the most important thing is that Juliette was born healthy. Who really cares what the doctor said, or that the childbirth experience I outlined in my birth plan wasn't to be? We survived, and that isn't a given.

But I did care. I cared enough to weep about it for weeks. Benjamin was bewildered. I refused to believe that my obsession with that little phrase was anything other than righteous anger, though I was clearly sporting a textbook case of the baby blues, if not full-fledged postpartum depression.

We learned quickly that Juliette was a screamer. Is a screamer. When she was only a day old, she got blistering mad about diaper changes. She gasped for breath and transfigured her sweet face into a pomegranate seed, shiny and red. Her fusses for milk were downright wrathful.

In my postpartum haze, I pondered if Dr. Hernandez might be the culprit. Just as the bitter Maleficent cursed Aurora with a fatal allergy to spinning wheels, Dr. Hernandez afflicted Juliette with constitutional anger; she'd made me angry, and my fury had transferred to my daughter.

The sheer irrationality of such a theory gives me pause. Perhaps I made something of a scapegoat out of Dr. Hernandez. She wasn't an exemplary obstetrician, and she definitely wasn't the right doctor for me. For months, I fixated on her many delivery room sins, convinced that she had left me emotionally and physically ravaged.

The term "scapegoat" has ancient scriptural origins. The Israelites used to drive a goat into the wilderness on the Day of Atonement, believing that the goat carried all the sins of the people on his back. He was a lightning rod for all their guilt, and the recipient of the punishment they deserved. I needed someone to blame for the way my life had been turned inside out, and I certainly didn't want to blame my innocent little girl. Without a doubt, Juliette had a far greater impact on my mind and body than the doctor who delivered her.

I was left with expected and crooked gratitude for Dr. Hernandez. I'd like to think I would never direct my resentment at Juliette, but thanks to her, I wasn't even tempted to do so. I had a perfect target in my imperfect doctor.

And I accomplished the equivalent of casting out the goat: I got a new doctor. Again.

4

Take and Eat

Summertime, Georgia. I was standing at the center of a gorgeous wood-paneled university chapel. The worship space was the first place I'd been all day that wasn't sweltering or air-conditioned enough to feel like a refrigerator. I had agreed to distribute the bread during the Lord's Supper, but at the altar the celebrant handed me the chalice full of Welch's grape juice. I'd never held the communion cup before, and as a cerebral seminarian fresh out of Major Christian Doctrines, I was mulling over the theological implications of blood atonement as I awkwardly mumbled " . . . the cup of salvation" to each communicant.

I was just getting into the swing of it, practically if not spiritually, when a young conference participant approached me with her arms crossed at the wrist in front of her heart. She wanted a blessing. I didn't catch on right away, even though I knew what it meant to cross one's arms at the communion table. I'd done it myself during mass at Roman Catholic churches. I just couldn't reconcile that this woman wanted *me* to bless her. I froze. She peered at me, her chin resting on the cradle of her crossed wrists, and whispered, "Will you bless me?" I nodded and, glad that she closed her eyes, pressed two fingers from my right hand to her forehead—having no clue what a protocol blessing entails—and silently pretended to bless her. Once it seemed as though a sufficient amount of time to impart a blessing passed, I tapped her on the shoulder like a kid playing Heads Up Seven Up, and she returned to her pew.

For months, I couldn't stop thinking about the woman. I tried to pray for her, but I didn't really know how to do that, either. I imagined myself in her shoes: full of expectation that the woman holding the chalice would be a conduit of God's own blessing. I fretted that she'd discerned I was a fraud. Worse, I considered the superstitious prospect that my phony blessing might actually have done more harm than good. Sometimes I wondered if I really did bless her—if just pretending with all my good intentions was enough.

***

Juliette came home from the hospital on a Saturday in January, the first clear morning after days of storms. Benjamin took every turn slowly, compulsively checking the rear view mirror to confirm that the sleeping baby was still present and in one piece. I was grateful that my mother didn't have to fly back to Ohio until after the weekend. We needed an adult around. Not only were we still fuzzy on the particulars of infant care; I was sore, exhausted, and scared out of my mind. Benjamin didn't have any postpartum wounds, but he was enduring his winter migraine season.

The newborn was clearly hungry. The watery colostrum that had begun leaking from my nipples the last few weeks of my pregnancy wasn't satisfying her. She took it upon herself to expedite the delivery of the real milk, demanding to nurse every hour, on the hour. She started with some polite rooting, an action that never ceased to remind me of a baby sparrow beseeching his mother for earthworms. If we didn't get my breast in her face promptly, she accelerated to an unrelenting scream within seconds.

It was all so *mammalian*.

Juliette hit liquid gold during her first marathon feeding in the black and white polka-dotted rocking chair. We struggled to get situated; I'd held her like a football in the hospital bed, but it seemed like she would pitch off the arm of the chair if I tried to run the same play in the comfort of our own nursery. She was frantic by the time she finally latched on, and I assumed that the feverish feeling in my breasts was pure sympathy. Nope. To claim that my milk "came in" sounds like such an understatement. My milk *stormed* in. By the end of the first feeding she was sputtering.

The onslaught of milk was overwhelming, and not just for Juliette. Within hours I was sporting a rack that surpassed the girth of grapefruits and challenged the volume of cantaloupes. My mother had the gall to comment, "My goodness, Juliette drinks from large milk jugs." I sent her to the supermarket for bags of frozen peas to relieve the pain of the swift expansion of my chest and ordered her back again for family-sized bags when the standard size failed to cover enough territory.

Oh, the pain. Nursing provided a whole spectrum of pain. There was the heated ache of fullness, the clogged ducts that throbbed like bruises, and most of all, the excruciating sting of being sucked on. The first thirty seconds of every feeding were almost unbearable. I often chanted, "Frick! Frick! Frick!" because it was the only word that remotely addressed the sharpness of the sensation. Nipples are, by nature, extraordinarily sensitive. It's what makes them so fun in certain situations. That hypersensitivity does not come in so handy when they are the membrane between the newborn and her milk. Over time they develop calluses, but not before a few weeks of small-scale suffering. It isn't uncommon for nipple skin to crack in the early days of breastfeeding. The consequent bloodletting is only really considered a problem if it makes the baby vomit.

There are potential complications. My clogged milk ducts never developed into mastitis, but a friend awoke in the middle of the night with an infection that she swears was twice as agonizing as labor. Some babies have a hard time latching onto the breast; some breasts have a hard time making enough milk. But the most common nursing complication is simply doing it wrong. One would think that something so natural would come naturally. One would be mistaken.

After ten days of pain no amount of lanolin balm could soothe, I began to suspect that something was amiss. I dreaded every feeding and considered unsealing the formula canisters we'd stashed in the top cupboard. (Mixed message alert: the hospital purportedly encouraged breastfeeding but dutifully passed out the formula company swag at discharge time.) I woke up on a Saturday morning determined to get some help. The local breastfeeding clinic opened at ten. First come, first served. Excellent.

Except it was not excellent. Benjamin had developed another migraine. His migraines are much more than mere headaches;

occasionally, his brain gets so flustered by the pain that it starts mimicking stroke symptoms. He was completely out of commission, and I was terrified to take Juliette out on my own. I hadn't even walked her around the block yet. I don't think I'd even walked *myself* around the block yet. Leaving the house on my own with an infant was enough to set off a panic attack, which is why I never so much as entertained the thought.

We didn't have a lot of friends in town, and my usual go-to girl had also just given birth. So I pulled out the church directory and called the chair of the board.

Phyllis retired from the Los Angeles Unified School District after a long career in the classroom and principal's office. If she ran her elementary school the way she ran the congregational board meetings, I can only imagine how greatly the superintendent—and the teachers—lamented her retirement. She is a fantastic leader: efficient, skillful, whip smart about both policies and people. She is reserved but warm, discreet but generous. I adore her, though she is not the kind of person who enjoys being publicly adored. I don't think she's the kind of woman who uses the word "adore," although she actively practices the verb in regard to her grandchildren—and Juliette.

Phyllis listened to my brief and teary explanation and promised to be there in twenty minutes. She made it in fifteen. As I introduced her to Juliette, I gushed with a sort of frenetic cheerfulness that only thinly obscured how close I was to losing my mind. Benjamin unfolded himself from the fetal position and peeled himself off the bathroom floor long enough to thank her for coming to rescue us.

We were the first ones to make it to the clinic just as Barbara, the lactation specialist, opened the doors. She ushered us into the consultation room. I declined Phyllis's offer to wait in the lobby. It was probably a huge violation of pastoral boundaries to drag a church member into a room in which my unsheathed breasts were going to be the main attraction. I was too wrecked to care. I desperately wanted my mother, and she was two thousand miles away. Phyllis was a remarkably good stand-in. I trusted her enough to know that not only could she handle the unorthodox intimacy, but she would continue to regard me as her pastor once I was ready to step back into the role.

It should be noted that not every pastor is so lucky—so blessed—to have a chair of the board like Phyllis in her corner.

The consult was brief, helpful, and moderately eventful. I learned that Juliette indeed sucked really hard—and not idiomatically. She had a strong jaw and a voracious appetite. Barbara weighed her before and after she nursed for five minutes on one breast and was amazed by the volume of milk she ingested. Barbara also noted that I wasn't properly directing my nipple into Juliette's mouth and was just leaning forward to give me some pointers when I accidentally squirted a thick stream of milk right between her eyes. Barbara and Phyllis laughed so hard I couldn't help but join in.

Maybe it was the nursing-induced oxytocin kicking in, but I walked out of that clinic flooded with love and gratitude for those women, and for the baby in my arms who suddenly seemed a little less like an inflictor of pain and a lot more like my daughter.

***

Sometimes it feels like all I've done since becoming a mother is pretend with good intentions. The love isn't pretense, not at all. And it's not like I don't have resources—internal reserves of intuition, a shelf of parenting books, and women like my mother, my sisters, Phyllis, and Barbara. I have a husband who, while excused from all breastfeeding responsibilities for biological reasons, truly is fully engaged in parenting when he isn't in the throes of a migraine. Still, no matter how I add it all up, it doesn't make me a mother. Only Juliette makes me a mother, and she showed up one day just expecting me to know how to bless her. My desperation to make breastfeeding work was rooted in my longing to have a tangible means to do so—a means as tangible as bread and wine. So long as the milk gets from my breast to her belly, I know she is receiving the blessing she needs. That her blessing pained me for a time . . . well, yes. That's how it works. Long after I first wrestled with those doctrines in classrooms and chapels, I've finally learned that there's no way for the bread to be broken and the wine to be spilled without someone's body and blood taking a hit. It isn't that the pain is redemptive. The pain is redeemed.

Take and eat, my daughter. This deluge of milk is called forth by you, and given for you.

5

The Hemorrhaging Woman

I was scheduled to be back in the pulpit at church exactly four weeks after Juliette was born. Shortly after I began my ministry at South Bay Christian Church, the governing board adopted a parental leave policy that afforded six weeks of paid leave. Their policy was a far greater benefit than many women receive, but if we're going to be completely honest about what a huge physical and emotional event having a baby is, *six weeks is not a whole lot.* I accidentally sacrificed two of my allotted weeks when, having fully succumbed to the awkwardness and discomfort of late pregnancy, I jumped the gun. Absolutely certain we would be home with a newborn by week's end, I dialed our guest preacher on Epiphany Sunday and asked him to start his interim ministry early. I was incapable of doing anything but gestate and nest, and I was carrying so low that every time I stood up I had the weirdest sensation that the kid was going to plumb fall out. Instead, she undropped. She bounced off the nethermost lining of my uterus and propelled herself back up to my rib cage, as far from the exit sign as could be. A retired high school teacher pointed this out after worship on my last day of work, claiming that his many years of counseling pregnant cheerleaders had made him an expert on such matters. "Oh, it will be another two weeks, no doubt about it," he said breezily. I wanted to smack him upside the head with my stale coffee cake but settled for vowing to myself I would prove him wrong.

I didn't, though not for lack of trying. Sadly, sheer force of will does not activate labor contractions.

So it was that the first two weeks of my maternity leave were spent prematernity. Though Juliette was only a week late, "only a week late" is roughly equivalent to seventeen eternities at that stage of pregnancy. My doctor was threatening to induce, my mother was scheduled to fly back to Ohio, and every moment was one less moment to heal and hold my daughter before being expected to function as a minister of Word and Sacrament again. Could anyone blame me for downing a glass of orange juice laced with castor oil? Now there's a cocktail that generates contractions. And (pregnant ladies should be warned if considering such drastic measures) bowel movements. Castor oil does not discriminate; anything and everything in your system will be expelled within hours.

The church arranged for me to have one additional Sunday off, giving me five weeks from Juliette's birthday to put myself back together again. I could have tacked on another week or two of vacation, but I felt a responsibility to come back. Perhaps I merely suffered from an exaggerated sense of self-importance, but when you pastor a tiny congregation—heck, when you *belong* to a tiny congregation—the impact of your presence and absence is weighted. I knew they couldn't afford for me to call in and ask for an extension. Even that one additional Sunday of time off wasn't covered by the operating budget; a member aware of the situation just kicked in an extra hundred and fifty bucks to pay the guest preacher. I didn't ruminate on the infinitely more humane family leave customs common in European nations or envy my ministry colleagues who nabbed three-month stays from church duties. Truth is, even if I'd wanted to cultivate a healthy resentment, I didn't have time. The five weeks went by at an alarming clip, especially since two of them were obscured by excruciating back pain. I learned the hard way that my chronically touchy lumbar couldn't handle the strain of babywearing.

I knew my maternity leave had been too brief when I realized that I would still be hemorrhaging when I led my first postpartum worship service. Granted, by then it was just a trickle. I'd preached while menstruating before and certainly didn't harbor any hidden fidelities to the Book of Leviticus prohibitions against "unclean" women. Though on further thought, maybe a lengthy exile from ritual and public life isn't such a terrible idea. It sounded moderately appealing in Anita Diamant's novel of feminist biblical midrash, *The Red Tent*. But the likelihood that I could get away with pitching a tent in the parsonage yard and holing up with my newborn and a handful of my closest girlfriends was nil, so back to work I went—though not without a nod to my condition. I've always loved hiding little allusions in my sermon manuscripts that no one but I would recognize—bits of favorite song lyrics, private connotations, inside jokes that are so well camouflaged you'd never guess the reason for the twinkle in my eye. It was no mere coincidence that in the introduction to my sermon about Jesus healing a blind man, I referred to another character healed by the Great Physician: the bleeding woman who grasped the hem of Jesus' garment and begged him to make her well.

It wasn't an inside joke so much as a cry for help.

The blood flow was minor. Normal. Lochia often lasts as long as six weeks after childbirth. But the flow was such a symbol of how vulnerable, how wounded I felt. It wasn't enough that I was sleep-deprived, that Juliette got first dibs on our nutrition co-op, or that my body was still a foreign landscape. I was *bleeding*.

And, by the end of the service, I was leaking another bodily fluid. Thank God for quadruple layers: nursing pads, bra, blouse, robe. Juliette was irate as Benjamin passed her off to me after the benediction. She'd refused the bottle of breast milk I'd pumped, so we fled to the rocking chair in the newly repurposed bride's room. Her needs were so immediate, so physical. The customary coffee-hour conversations would have to wait until next Sunday.

When I fretted to a member about the quality of my work in those first weeks back, she chuckled, saying that all I needed to do was display the baby on the marble communion table. Everyone would be perfectly content to contemplate new life for an hour, until it was time to regroup at the local diner for eggs and bacon. *Sure*, I thought. *Until the new life starts screaming. Or pooping.*

***

My sister had warned me that I would have to relearn how to do everything after becoming a mother. *Everything*. Truer words have never been spoken. Eating presented one of the larger challenges; Juliette demanded to be held every waking moment (as well as many of her sleeping ones), so I learned to prop her up on a pillow and pray that if I did drop marinara sauce on her, it wouldn't land in her nose.

I knew that I wasn't exactly going to hit the ground running when I went back to work, especially because Juliette came with me. I was grateful that we didn't have to be separated quite yet, except that I hadn't written a sermon in a really long time. (If you ever find yourself in the position of going on maternity leave too early, consider getting a head start on your first major postbaby project instead of watching entire seasons of *Desperate Housewives* on DVD, for example.) Last time I checked, I was one of those writers who demanded the perfect balance of silence, procrastination, inspiration, long stretches of time, and a general lack of irresistibly cute distractions in order to commit a single word to the page. Oh, and back in the day I was pretty hooked on having two hands with which to type the aforementioned word. I hear that the longest word you can type one-handed is "stewardesses," but I really don't think I could get away with preaching a manuscript that just repeats the politically incorrect term for flight attendants, even if I did wave a newborn baby in my parishioners' faces as a distraction.

Since our early marital conversations, we knew that if we ever did have a kid, Benjamin would be the one to step out of the workforce and stay home—and not just because it's hard to argue that it is appropriate to continue living at one's church-owned home if one is no longer working for said church. Benjamin is famously good with children; he has attained celebrity status with his nieces and nephews because he is so much fun. Whenever we visit family, I wear out after fifteen or twenty minutes of hide-and-seek or Chutes and Ladders. It takes me a good hour of reading literary fiction on the sofa to recover enough for a rematch. Benjamin, on the other hand, is tireless. He wears the kids out. They take champion naps when we're in town (which is why he has also attained celebrity status with my sisters). He wanted to stay home with our daughter, and while it seems so blunt to put it this way, I didn't. My sense of vocation goes something like this: I must be actively engaged in ministry or I will shrivel up and die. He doesn't feel that way about his career in social services. He likes the work, he's good at it, but "job coach for people with developmental disabilities" isn't tattooed on his soul the way "pastor" is on mine.

Hence, the plan: I would bring the baby with me to the church office while he finished up his final commitments at work. I didn't dare schedule any pastoral visits in those first weeks back, and I'm especially grateful that no one died. The likelihood that my hormones would get the better of me and the poor shut-in or bereaved family would be stuck with a weeping minister was far too steep. I didn't even dare wear mascara until Juliette was eight months old.

At the end of Benjamin's two-week notice, he would take over from there, more or less. Our checking account demanded that he drum up a part-time job, and though it meant even more changes and even greater challenges, it also seemed like a good time for him to finish his long-abandoned bachelor's degree. The naïve plan was to figure out a way to tag-team Juliette's care until she was at least a year old. However his schedule panned out, I was pretty sure I could fill in the gaps. Thankfully, the busyness of ministry is matched only by its flexibility. There's no clock to punch in pastoral ministry (and if there is, someone needs to call a Pastoral Relations Committee meeting, stat). No one cared if I crafted the worship liturgy in my church study or, as would soon become my practice, propped up on pillows in bed with the napping infant swaddled against my chest. I'd been told that there are few better jobs than ministry—especially ministry in a small congregation—for being a working mama. It's true. The whole congregation was rooting for us.

I survived the first week. I wrote the sermon, cute distractions and all. I preached it, private allusions and all. I fled the scene, screeching baby and all. And then on the first day of my second week back, our part-time church secretary gave notice.

Did I mention that my husband was looking for part-time work?

They say God works in mysterious ways.

It was a terrible and terrific idea all at once. The personnel committee interviewed Benjamin for the position (which was inexplicably renamed office manager, because apparently women can be pastors but men can't be secretaries). He was offered the job and, after extensive hemming and hawing ("One more time . . . who is going to watch Juliette when we are both at church?"), he accepted.

And thus it was: my marriage started hemorrhaging just as my body finally stopped.

6

The Passions

I found it while sorting through a box of pictures on a Sunday afternoon. The pictures were disorganized, just the way I like them: a jumble of images that roughly mimicked the way memories drift through one's mind. I snatched it from the pile, a chill creeping down my spine. *Who the hell took this?* In the picture, I am sitting at the kitchen table in our seminary campus apartment. My shoulders are hunched, my hands partially obscuring my anguished face. Benjamin is standing nearby, his face contorted with anger, his hands raised into the air in a posture of pure fury. I stared at it, stupidly, for a full minute before I remembered. We had not been in the throes of a fight. We were pretending. My best friend from Ohio had taken the photograph. She was visiting for the weekend, and we'd taken her to the J. Paul Getty Museum perched in the hills north of Los Angeles. We were all drawn to the special exhibit, *Bill Viola: The Passions*. In the digital portraits—some subtly moving, thanks to newfangled flat-screen technology—actors embodied a range of emotions: joy, sadness, grief, anger. After dinner, between bursts of hysterical laughter, we recreated the scenes. There is no better icon for our marriage than the image Lisa captured: the rousing good time all but obscured by the all-too-familiar anguish and anger. I couldn't decide if I wanted to tear it up or frame it.

***

"Why don't you just let me do it?" An innocuous question, right? Especially when delivered in such a light—almost airy!—tone of voice. The new church office manager should have been pleased that I was offering to take over one of the items on his to-do list. Why wouldn't he simply cease and desist his misguided efforts to complete the requested revisions to the monthly newsletter and, I don't know . . . sort junk mail? Rock the baby? Anything but further screw up the layout I had so painstakingly designed.

Benjamin pushed his secretary chair away from the desk. One of the casters bumped my toe; I let out an exaggerated gasp to make sure he knew I had been injured. So what if I wasn't *really* hurt or that my feet would have been out of range of his vicious wheels if I hadn't been hovering.

He didn't apologize. I handed over a sleeping Juliette, sank into his seat, and with the slightest hint of showmanship, expertly clicked around Microsoft Publisher until the article text wrapped neatly around the denominational mission logo. I glanced over the desk at Benjamin. He had propped Juliette up on his shoulder in a way that, from my humble perspective, looked uncomfortable to both of them. "Are you sure you're supporting her head?"

He sighed. "She's fine." There was no lightness or air in his response. His words were defensive, his tone spent.

"What's wrong?" I asked, again with feigned innocence. My trademark. It was all part of the script we stuck to, day after demoralizing day. His next line would be some sort of denial that anything is wrong, though the words would be so dissonant with his entire countenance. I would be compelled to press for an honest answer. He would resist. Finally, I would break him. He would explode into a litany of grievances, most of which were at least partly true. I micromanaged both his church work and his parenting. I relentlessly nagged him beyond his ability to brush it off. I swore I was supportive of his decision to finish his bachelor's degree, but I was passive-aggressive about how much his classes inconvenienced my work schedule.

These complaints—all of which I had heard many times before—were occasionally accompanied by inexcusable insults. Once, while staying at my parents' house for a family reunion, we realized that a particularly bitter exchange had been broadcast, via baby monitor, to the back porch. If we hadn't been so humiliated—if I hadn't felt like I had just been verbally slammed against that deep abyss known as rock bottom, if Benjamin hadn't felt like he'd yet again become the person he most did not wish to be—we might have chuckled at how easily the episode could be adapted into a situation comedy. To this day, we don't know if my sisters told the truth or if they were merely pretending that they hadn't heard the words that reduced me to hysterical sobs and inspired a web search for local divorce lawyers.

The drama ended, without fail, when Benjamin came to his senses and offered a horrified and heartfelt apology. I always said that I was sorry too, but my apologies were insincere. Whatever wrongs I committed were swept away by his overreaction. It was extraordinarily convenient, really. I was never forced to acknowledge my part in the dysfunction because I was absolved by merit of being the identifiable victim. Meanwhile, my husband buried himself under yet another layer of self-loathing.

Repeat.

***

Even before he beguiled the congregation with his stay-at-home-dad gig, my husband was a beloved figure at church. It pleased me that folks at church seemed to "get" Benjamin. Not everyone does, thanks to the trace of social anxiety that inhibits his capacity for small talk. If you take the time to get to know him, you discover that my husband is passionate, principled, sensitive, humble, and wickedly funny. If you are lucky enough to be related to him by blood or law, you know that he is vividly all those things. Although he refuses to sing in public—not even when his tenor voice would be concealed within the din of a congregation—at home, he shuffles through a whole repertoire of songs: songs for Juliette, songs for washing the dishes, songs for annoying his wife, and songs to herald the Cleveland Browns, his beloved football team. Maybe he would be just another avid Cleveland fan if his mother hadn't been on their secretarial staff for over twenty years, if his grandmother hadn't been the head of the stadium concessions department, or if Bernie Kosar hadn't called him "Opie" the summer he worked as a ball boy. At the start of every football season, he convinces himself that they will win the Super Bowl—such optimism in the face of their interminably abysmal record is remarkable. His affinity for the Browns is revealing. To tell the story of the Browns, you have to use words like *loyalty, betrayal, hope, failure, disappointment*; you need the same vocabulary for Benjamin's story. While I know little in life could make him happier than actually witnessing the Browns score the winning touchdown on the first Sunday in February, it would reorder his universe to pledge allegiance to anything but an underdog. Still, the word you long to add to the biography of the team and their biggest fan is *redemption*.

Like many troubled marriages, ours looked dandy from the outside. I appeared to be the rare mother who got to "have it all," working at a demanding but fulfilling job without the obligatory guilt; my kid didn't get schlepped to daycare for forty hours a week, but was cared for by her own father. Benjamin was appraised a hero, selflessly sacrificing career advancement for the sake of his family. The only way we could have been a more traditional pastor/spouse combination was if, in addition to staying home with the newborn, coordinating the men's fellowship group, and preparing the weekly worship bulletins, he plopped down at the piano and accompanied the hymns on Sunday mornings. I'm grateful that he dropped out of piano lessons in elementary school.

We carpooled to church three mornings a week. Benjamin drove, and I sat in the backseat next to Juliette, our lunchbox of cheese and apples and homemade bread on my lap. There was something so wholesome and hopeful about those commutes to church, both of us convinced that this was the day we would be released from our destructive patterns—except on the days when the bickering began before we even crossed the threshold of the parsonage. I wish I knew why we were infected with the same naïveté and pride. Between the two of us, we were teeming with indignation. For something frequently connected to righteousness, ours was pure poison. Once at a salon while I was still a seminary student, I chatted with the colorist while she bleached my highlights to a perfect shade of platinum. She was fascinated by my intended vocation, and when I disclosed that my husband was employed in social work, she swooned. "Your house must be so peaceful, such good people living together!" I cringed at her grossly mistaken assumption. Although our new roles as parents and colleagues had propelled us into a full-blown crisis, the fights weren't new. They had always erupted between moments of hilarity and joy and tenderness. Now, they were crowding out the shining moments.

One Saturday afternoon when an outing to the beach—*the beach!*—was thwarted by yet another monumental blow up, Benjamin parked the car along a palm-lined residential street. Juliette, not yet six months old, had been lulled to sleep by the movement of the Hyundai, a small solace given the racket we'd generated. I remember nothing about the fight and little about the solemn conversation that followed, except that it was the first in which we seriously discussed the possibility of separating. With the same lips that we had used to consummate our first kiss and to declare our marital vows, we tested out the word *divorce*. We couldn't survive much longer without separate living quarters or a miracle. The former would break our hearts, and the latter was so long overdue we could only assume it had been remaindered.

With divorce on the table and divine help beyond our reach, we agreed: it was time to seek professional help.

One of my oldest tricks was to threaten to sign us up for marriage counseling. I didn't actually mean it. It was one of many things I sputtered in the midst of heated quarrels. I detested the vision of us sitting on opposite ends of an ugly sofa in some musty office, paying ungodly amounts of money for the privilege of dissecting our doomed marriage with a stranger. No matter that as a Christian I supposedly believed in the possibility of transformation and healing or that as a pastor I had received modest training in the craft of pastoral counseling—a craft that, at the level of congregational ministry, mostly entails listening and referring people to credentialed therapists. I didn't think counseling could make a difference, an illogical counterweight to my ragged optimism that we could change of our own volition.

We put a call in to Dr. Scar, a Missouri Synod Lutheran minister and psychotherapist whose number I kept in my top desk drawer to distribute to other people. (And, yes, that really is his name.) I sent Benjamin to the first appointment alone because—and now I laugh—I was convinced that he was the problem. If he could learn to control his temper, we'd be fine. Perhaps there is no better proof that I, too, was a problem. *I had the audacity to believe I could sit out marriage counseling.* It didn't take long for Dr. Scar to call me out and invite me in. So it was that we added a fourth morning commute to our week. The nine miles to the Good Samaritan Counseling Center never felt wholesome or hopeful, but more akin to reporting for orthodontic work. Friday after Friday—truly a charmer of a way to spend one's only day off. Just as I'd imagined, we sat on an ugly sofa in a musty office, hashing out intimate inadequacies in the presence of an outsider . . . an outsider who was perceptive, challenging, infuriating, and brilliant.

The months passed and our slow progress compounded into noticeable change. I'm amazed that a marriage devoid of infidelity and physical violence could be so damaged, that two people who were so functional could be so broken. But I'm even more amazed that such damage could be mended and such brokenness healed. We aren't cured, but we have changed, thanks to counseling, hard work, and yes, beyond a shadow of doubt, divine intervention. We hadn't even realized it and likely would have rolled our eyes if anyone pointed it out, but we were white-knuckling the hem of Jesus' garment all throughout the trying journey.

***

Like a lot of pastors, I have a boilerplate sermon I pull out and adapt for most of the weddings I officiate. I don't do it because I'm too lazy to write a new one or get to know the bride and groom. I don't care for hyperpersonalized wedding homilies that waste precious time recounting the story of how the couple met. Let the best man tell how it really went down in his drunken toast. I bear the responsibility of binding people together, legally and spiritually, and it's my last chance to dole out my finest counsel. I preach the same wedding sermon again and again because I believe it. I quote Dietrich Bonhoeffer, who said, "It is not love that sustains your marriage, but marriage that sustains your love." I officiated a wedding at the height of my own marriage emergency. My heart ached as I rehearsed the climactic paragraph, the sideways blessing promising the couple that as they nurture their marriage with time, prayers, and faithfulness to the breadth and depth of their wedding vows, their love will become ever richer, ever deeper. I remind them they marry because they love one another, but by the grace of God, they will love one another because they are married. And then I utter the grandiose statement that may or may not be a lie: that the covenant of marriage will give their love the muscle it needs to persist, to forgive, and to actually live faithfully together in plenty and in want, in joy and in sorrow, and in sickness and in health. The best I could hope, I guess, was that the couple might be stubborn enough to find out if it could be true. That was the best I hoped for us, some days.

***

Not to perpetuate the myth that having a child can save a marriage, but the other thing that saved our marriage was having a child. Our daughter alone wouldn't have been enough; there's no question we needed Dr. Scar and the Holy Spirit. On paper, it looks like Juliette's birth actually exacerbated an already borderline relationship. She was born in January, and we were in counseling by July. But the baby didn't generate the trouble; she was the impetus for finally doing something about it. We'd put up with an ailing marriage for over five years, and suddenly, there was a small person whose life would be radically altered if we couldn't pull it together. We hadn't done it for ourselves, but we would do anything for her.

A year into counseling, she invented a game that, despite its joyous premise, made me unspeakably sad. Benjamin and I were sitting in opposite corners of the den. Juliette ran back and forth across the length of the room, laughing and cooing and giving us hugs. I caught a glimpse of another outcome, in which my daughter spent her life trouncing between parents, her greetings dogged by imminent farewells. I couldn't bear it. I got up and walked across the room to sit next to my husband. He took my hand as if he understood. He probably did; my husband is an extraordinary man. I kissed him, even as Juliette noisily protested that I'd ruined her game.

Just as alcoholics are perpetually in recovery, so too are we. But ours is a story that only needs one more word to be true: *redemption*. As for the Cleveland Browns, maybe next year. This year's already shot.

7

Saved by the Childbearing

When Juliette was five months old, I received an invitation to participate in a clergy panel in the local newspaper. I knew going in that I would probably be the odd one out; though I was anything but a regular reader of the moderately conservative rag, I'd sifted through the Saturday edition at Starbucks enough times during my premotherhood days to know that their clergy panels were generally peopled by middle-aged evangelical pastors who were, without exception, of the male gender. I rather liked the idea of shaking things up, and Lord knows my tiny and beloved congregation could use some free publicity. I signed on, even though it meant that I had to submit my first one-hundred-and-fifty-word response within less than a day's turnaround—not an easy task, given that the opportunity arose during Benjamin's first week of summer school. The question was dumb, but I pretended it wasn't, dashing off as intelligent and faithful a response as I could muster. The morning it hit the stands, we strapped Juliette into her stroller, filled our pockets with quarters, and ambled down to the nearest newspaper kiosk. Sure enough, I sang "One of These Things (Is Not Like the Others)" on the way home.

I saw the second question coming a mile away. The campaign to prohibit same-sex marriage in California was winding up, second only to the political frenzy over the presidential campaign. I painstakingly chiseled out an answer that was careful but honest, explaining that the members of my church must agree on only one essential: that Jesus Christ is the Son of God and that he is our Lord and Savior. Beyond that, we interpret the Bible according to our own consciences, and our opinions about human sexuality are accordingly all over the board. Knowing full well that our relative obscurity made us unlikely to gain much traction in the gay community, I promised that my church would prayerfully and respectfully discern how to respond to same-sex couples seeking the covenant of marriage and that in any case we would continue to be a church where all people were joyfully welcomed.

Only one parishioner questioned my answer; she thought I should have just come out and said what I thought. For the most part, though, my people seemed to think I hadn't made a complete fool of myself (or them) in the local paper. I think they were just glad I hadn't come across as a homophobic fundamentalist, like my panel mates. Having avoided conflict without totally selling out my own opinion (which is, for the record, that same-sex relationships are less of a threat to marriage and society as a whole than, say, divorce. *Mazel Tov!*), I fielded the next couple of questions with tolerance, diplomacy, and measurably less anxiety. Thankfully, the newspaper also dialed down the aggressive controversy seeking. When the last of my three weeks of panel duty hit the press, I didn't even remember to snag a copy; one of my sweet church ladies slipped me a clipping after worship the next week.

Benjamin had taken Juliette down to the library so I could spend some precious solitary moments engaged in the kind of thinking that just didn't happen with a baby in the office. Early that fall, we were heading to the local Roman Catholic retreat center for an all-church retreat, and I was determined to not throw together a plan at the last minute. I was absorbed by my new manual for leading spiritual retreats when the phone rang. I almost didn't pick it up. Most church members called me on my cell phone if they needed to speak to me; midafternoon calls usually took the form of solicitations, such as Christian businesses in Texas wanting us to spend money we didn't have on a youth group we didn't have. But I took the call, if only to avoid listening to the interminably long answering machine message featuring my girlish voice optimistically supplying information about Sunday's services. I always answered the phone in the manner I had learned was most efficient: "South Bay Christian Church—this is Pastor Katherine." Once I fielded a call from a colleague, a middle-aged man who would have fit in swimmingly with my newspaper pals but for his ultraliberal theology and politics. Without even saying "hello," he responded, "Do you really call yourself that?" in utter disbelief. Yes, I do call myself Pastor Katherine—at least when I answer the telephone—because if I don't, the cold caller will immediately ask to speak to the pastor. The caller will then inevitably be a little ruffled when he or she is told the pastor is speaking. I mentally retorted, *I don't suppose anyone mistakes you for the secretary,* but chose instead to swallow my indignation and move on with the conversation.

The man on the other end of this call apparently missed the verbal cue. "May I please speak to your pastor?"

I pleasantly reiterated that I was the pastor of the church; I asked what I could do for him. He clearly wasn't calling to sell me something; perhaps he was contacting me for help with paying for a hotel room or a tank of gas, or maybe even for information about joining the church.

"I'm confused," he said, the sarcasm so thick I could recognize it even in the voice of a total stranger. "You're the pastor?"

As it turned out, I was speaking to someone who had spotted me in the newspaper and was so passionate about his conviction that I should not be a pastor (and that all my opinions were hogwash) that he tracked me down to tell me so.

I noted that Paul wrote in his letter to the Galatians, "There is no longer Jew or Greek, there is no longer slave or free, there is no longer male and female; for all of you are one in Christ Jesus" (3:28). He reminded me that Paul also wrote in his first letter to Timothy, "I permit no woman to teach or to have authority over a man; she is to keep silent" (2:12).

Then I argued that Mary Magdalene was the first person called to preach on Easter Sunday, that Jesus himself ordained her to go and tell the other disciples that he would meet them in Galilee. Not that the men listened to her, but she did her part by proclaiming the astounding news that Jesus Christ is risen. He quoted 1 Corinthians 14:34–35, where Paul commands, "Women should be silent in the churches. For they are not permitted to speak, but should be subordinate, as the law also says. If there is anything they desire to know, let them ask their husbands at home. For it is shameful for a woman to speak in church."

At that point I changed tactics and reminded him that slavery—of all things, *slavery*—is affirmed as an acceptable practice in the New Testament. Perhaps this business of relegating women to second-class citizens is another sign of the historical context out of which these sacred scriptures emerged.

And it went on and on, back and forth, and we succeeded in ripping the Holy Bible to shreds—these are my verses, those are yours, and we are anything but one in Christ Jesus. I tried to engage the caller in a mature discussion about biblical interpretation and historical context, but when it became clear that the last thing he wanted was a rational conversation, I got off the phone as quickly and politely as I could. And then I cried.

I did a quick inventory. One of my childhood pastors was female. As a teenager, some of my best mentors were female pastors. I went to seminary for three years (where many of my professors were ordained female clergywomen) and earned a Master of Divinity degree. My home church as well as the regional committee on ministry discerned that I have a call to ordained ministry. The General Minister and President of my denomination is a woman. My first church unanimously called me to be their first female solo pastor. I have a phenomenal support network of clergy friends, many of whom are women.

When I called upon that circle for a little encouragement, they lovingly echoed the voice of the Holy Spirit, confirming in a hundred different ways that God calls women into ministry and that God had called this woman into ministry.

I know that, of course. Though it came as a surprise to me (and probably the vast majority of people I knew in my youth), I'm clearly supposed to be doing what I do. I'm not the best, though I'm better than I thought I'd be. When I'm rattled by a tough pastoral visit, I dream about ensconcing myself in some ivory tower as a literature professor. When our bank account plateaus just south of comfort, I wonder just what it is lawyers do, anyway, and could I do it if it paid well enough? But my sense that this is the life to which God has called me is so strong it's enough to make me read the book of Jonah literally. There's no escaping pastoral ministry, and I really wouldn't want to if I could. And while it wasn't a primary reason I kept working after Juliette was born, it matters that my daughter witnesses me responding faithfully to my vocation.

And it is her watchful eyes that make me that much more indignant about—and that much more sensitive to—arbitrary nonsense about what girls can and can't do. I'm not the type to teach my daughter she can do anything she wants to do if she tries hard enough. It's an appealing sentiment, but it's not exactly true (for instance, if she inherits my math skills, her chances at becoming a mechanical engineer are totally shot). Neither does that line allow for the very real stirrings of the Spirit. Perhaps I'll tell her she can do anything God has in mind for her if she tries hard enough. What I can't abide by is anyone else telling her she can't do what God calls her to do. Or, for that matter, anyone telling me I can't do what God has called me to do.

I just couldn't quite shake the conversation. It haunted me for weeks. At first I heard the voice of the man, snide and condescending, rattling around in my head. But before long his voice was replaced by the voice of scripture, the sacred shared book that he had used against me. In particular, the verses from the first letter to Timothy lodged themselves in my mind:

> Let a woman learn in silence with full submission. I permit no woman to teach or to have authority over a man; she is to keep silent. For Adam was formed first, then Eve; and Adam was not deceived, but the woman was deceived and became a transgressor. Yet she will be saved through childbearing, provided they continue in faith and love and holiness, with modesty. (1 Tim. 2:11–15)

The passage alternately angered and fascinated me; I couldn't imagine how I'd been a Christian—a pastor—for so long without having ever seriously considered these words. My previous tack had been to simply ignore them, to write them off as culturally irrelevant drivel and as a sign that while the Bible may be inspired, it is far from inerrant. But when a passage gets stuck in my head, there's usually only one way to get it out: to proclaim it from the pulpit.

And that is how I came to preach a sermon about how I have no business preaching sermons. Naturally, that isn't exactly how it went down. I recounted the phone call (with many an incensed mur-mur from the pews), confessed my frustration with scriptures like these, and acknowledged the matter of cultural context. And then I focused on the strangest part of the scripture: its left-field emphasis on childbearing. When did Jesus ever teach that having babies saves women or that becoming a mother is tantamount to eternal salva-tion? What about our fundamental confession that Jesus saves? The punch line of the sermon was supplied by my favorite biblical com-mentary, which noted that in the original Greek, the scripture reads "women are saved through *the* childbearing"—which is supposed to be a pun for the birth of Jesus. Of course women are saved by the One born fully human and fully divine. So are men.

It was a happy ending to the sermon, a means of celebrating the presence of good news in a challenging and unpopular scripture. I think everyone left happy. But as I went home to my husband and my kid, I realized that I might have been a little too cavalier about throw-ing the baby out with the bathwater. Though it seems an affront to my feminism and my faith, it's true: I am one woman who has been saved—at least in part—by childbearing. Not just the childbearing that Mary undertook to bring the newborn Christ into the world, but the childbearing I did to bring the newborn Juliette into the world. Her birth opened something in me, and while that opening is a magnet for fear—and oh, what a risk it is to love so completely—it is also an invitation to greater faith, love, and holiness. But salvation will never cause me to be silent, not the redemption of my soul by Jesus or the rescuing of my spirit by Juliette.

I will preach this good news and sing in praise of all that saves. How could I not?

8

Elegance, Economy, Etymology

Nine months before our nuptials and six years before Juliette was conceived, Benjamin brought me a nosegay on our first date. We went to Tommy's, a vegetarian restaurant in Coventry Village, and then he took me to a bar. He explained on the way over that Mitzi Jerman's was a classic Cleveland landmark on St. Clair Avenue. Mitzi was born in the apartment above the establishment and worked there until shortly before she died a couple of years ago. The elderly legend herself was pouring the drinks that night, and what little of her showed from behind the tall counter was all but obscured by a cloud of cigarette smoke. I ordered first—club soda, which I do not like. I was shaking and couldn't think of anything else to say. I didn't know that much about my date except that he had red hair, wrote plainspoken poetry, and was an intermittently sober alcoholic. Later, he told me that he hadn't yet decided whether or not he would get a beer—he had been drinking the night before—but my club soda inspired him to order a Coke. We left as soon as we'd downed our sodas. I don't remember what we talked about, if anything. It is as though my memory only allowed one snapshot: the moment Benjamin did not order a drink.

I suggested Ben & Jerry's ice cream at his place. He didn't take me home until seven thirty the next morning. We slept in our clothes on his futon, after I waited so long for him to kiss me that we were too tired to drive across town, past all the Kent bars, to my apartment. He never did kiss me first; I got impatient and kissed him. He kissed back.

I already knew that I would marry him. That was the decision I made before I accepted the date. The logic was fuzzy and firm all at the same time. I didn't want to hurt him or be responsible for his further descent into drinking. I wanted to save him and be saved by him. I wanted to love and be loved by him.

Mere months after I reached the legal drinking age, I voluntarily gave up spirits for the benefit of my new boyfriend. If my solidarity shored up his resolve, then I could easily become a teetotaler. I had imagined for myself a life spiked with champagne toasts, microbrewed beers, perhaps even the occasional shot of celebratory whiskey. Instead, Benjamin slipped a ring on my finger, an amethyst set in silver filigree. Elegant, economical, but above all etymological. *Amethyst* derives from the Greek *a methyskein*. Not intoxicating. The ancients believed the violet quartz warded off drunkenness. I had no delusions that a lucky charm was any substitute for the twelve steps of Alcoholics Anonymous, but cherished the symbol. Our marriage was inextricably bound to his sobriety. My sobriety.

But neither the covenant nor the talisman could ward off temptation. I have gazed longingly at the wine aisle at Trader Joe's, wondering if the "Two Buck Chuck" is potable. I have scanned liquor shelves for labels I recognize from the handful of times I drank to intoxication. My cheeks flush with shame, as if I were eyeing not a bottle but another man. It has always seemed like a sign of personal immaturity. Obviously I would choose my husband over a glass of champagne. To long for something that poisoned his life is surely a violation of our relationship.

***

We had exchanged vague niceties for months. *Yeah, we should do something together . . . sometime. Let's plan something once we're all not so busy.* When Carla pulled her planner out of her knapsack in the library one day, I realized that she actually meant it. It wasn't that I didn't want to hang out with Carla and her boyfriend, Pete. I liked Carla. We had met the spring before we started seminary when we both visited campus the same weekend. All summer I'd assumed that she would be my primary friend, the one with whom I would compare notes on Kierkegaard and study for the Hebrew Bible oral examination. The night before classes started, she hosted a party on campus. Benjamin and I stopped by briefly, even though we knew there would be alcohol. The party itself was forgettable; my memory snapshot for that evening is reserved for the earthquake that happened just before midnight, when we were back in our apartment across the courtyard, half asleep in bed. Ever the Midwesterners, it took us a moment to figure out what had happened. Benjamin's first guess was that the seminarians had gotten rowdy and someone had drunkenly chucked a piece of furniture off the third floor balcony.

Carla, as it turned out, was not destined to be my seminary soul mate. I delivered myself from temptation—and envy—by distancing myself from her. I never tried to explain; I didn't know her that well, for one, and Benjamin was reluctant to broadcast that he was just shy of a year's sobriety. I simply didn't continue the friendship we both assumed would flourish. Yet there we were, two years after the hasty abortion of our nascent camaraderie, comparing calendars.

And there we were again, a week later, preparing a recovering alcoholic's nightmare of a dinner. Fondue, as it turns out, includes a lot of alcohol. Carla and Pete had brought over the fixings for beer-battered cauliflower, wine-infused cheese, and brandied chocolate sauce. I had called Carla the day before to mention that we didn't drink (with no explanation, leaving her to wonder what oddball brand of theologically liberal fundamentalists we might be), yet our countertops were cluttered with various and sundry bottles. In a gesture of respect, they didn't uncork any wine for the table.

To say the dinner party was a disaster is an understatement. The food was divine—I could live on fresh sourdough baptized in melted gruyere—but for Benjamin, it was a veritable funhouse with booze hiding in every course. He came home from work just as we were lighting the Sterno burners. I pretended not to see the look of betrayal on his face when he assessed the kitchen. He claimed to have eaten a big lunch. (Lie: he hadn't eaten since breakfast.) Throughout the meal, we patched together awkward conversation with Carla and Pete while I guiltily devoured his share of the feast.

We argued as soon as our guests took their leave. I lost the fight, and not just because the incursion of alcohol into the sanctuary of our apartment happened on my watch. I lost because even as I argued that a few ounces of wine mixed into the cheese sauce couldn't possibly intoxicate a person, my speech was slurred.

***

For nearly eight years, I walked in sober solidarity with Benjamin (save for the boozy cheese). Yet the July of Juliette's second year, while I was tucked away at an idyllic workshop about writing and the pastoral life, I poured myself a glass of wine. It smacked of infidelity, a sin against my husband. And yet, I drank: a half glass of Smoking Loon red, and a half glass of chardonnay. A consummation of frustrated desire, to be sure.

But I did not get tipsy against Benjamin's will (and yes, the equivalent of one glass of wine was all it took). Around the time Juliette learned to crawl, I confessed that I sometimes wished for a drink, that I daydreamed about observing the conclusion of breast-feeding with a toast. The admission startled and hurt him. To betray our shared sobriety would be to betray him. He would be left vulnerable . . . forced to sustain his temperance alone. The confession revealed that my sacrifice had become his crutch. Questions began to ferment. Was it really so healthy that his recovery was so tangled up in our marriage? Is sobriety that depends upon the restraint of another truly sobriety? Still, wouldn't it be a silly and unnecessary risk to change course now?

But soon enough, Benjamin did change course—or rather, gave me permission to do so if I so pleased. He released me from my pledge to abstain from alcohol, if the circumstances were right. For him, the right circumstances precluded drinking and driving (naturally), and excluded his presence. He could not abide my drinking in his company, but if I wanted to have a drink elsewhere, then I had his acquiescence, if not his blessing. I ruminated on this new information for months. Part of me wondered if it was, at least on some level, a test.

One of the lessons we learned in marriage counseling is that we have a tendency toward blurring the lines distinguishing one from another. In our quest for honesty and trust, we eliminated our sense of personal privacy. The shared policy of telling each other everything emerged from the shaky beginnings of our marriage, which were not particularly honest or trustworthy. The injuries we sustained from that era propelled us to the other pole. Yet we have realized that true intimacy is impossible without maintaining ourselves as two separate individuals, complete with private lives. Which isn't to say that we have begun a new era of secrecy. But a marriage is made of two people, not one mushed-together mess of codependency.

Still, why is it so hard for me to believe that if I drink, the alcohol doesn't travel to his bloodstream?

***

These days our kitchen is usually stocked with cabernet in the pantry and chardonnay in the refrigerator door. I toss my spent corks in a hand-thrown pottery bowl that sits alongside a dried nosegay on the windowsill over the sink. Invariably, the finer varieties were purchased not by me but by my faithfully sober spouse; I can't bring myself to spend more than seven dollars on something so fleeting as a bottle of wine, but Benjamin will spend twice as much for the joy of acquainting me with a new vintage. I still sometimes glance sideways at him when I fetch our solitary stemmed glass from the hutch—does he really mean it when he says it doesn't bother him anymore? But I'm quite sure he does. Somewhere along the line Benjamin realized that proximity to alcohol no longer feels like an emergency, so long as the alcohol doesn't touch his own lips. We have made the revolutionary discovery that *we are individuals.* Furthermore, he rather likes me after I've had a glass of wine. As it turns out, I'm a delightful drinker. Just a touch of alcohol makes me at least 25 percent more likely to laugh at dumb jokes and 50 percent more likely to make them. I'm somehow mellower and friskier all at the same time, and I sleep like our baby never did.

I drink alone but not alone. More often than not, when I have a drink in my left hand, the fingers of my right are interlaced with Benjamin's. If he needed me to sit beside him on the proverbial bandwagon again, I would flush my favorite spirits down the john and swallow my aspirations to become an amateur sommelier. But I would do it not as a crutch but as a friend, not as a codependent but as a coconspirator.

Until that day—if it ever comes—I'll keep raising my glass in honor of what's not in his.

9

Fear

Fear thrives in the face of the unknown. It is often beyond words and images; it is a physiological response to silence, darkness, and tomorrow. It is almost always about death. You can't live in fear, at least not for very long. But you have options. You can cope, you can flee, you can pray, and you can turn the lights on and make faces at the very monsters that threatened to extinguish you. Or, if you are of a particular temperament, you can fill in all the blanks with a tool that will scribble on the surface of any fear: anxiety.

Anxiety, too, thrives in the face of the unknown. Anxiety makes a graven image of it, artfully obscuring mystery with an infinite sketch of possible disasters. It leaves no potential tragedy unturned, no catastrophe unconceived. In the absence of certainty, anxiety assures that the worst will happen. Anxiety may save you from abject fear, but at a cost. It is exhausting. It is depressing. And it isn't just about death; it leads to death.

I am an anxious adult, and I was an anxious child. I could not bear to follow along as Alice descended into Wonderland; even after I learned the ending, I was sure she would not escape the surreal prison. Big changes wear my nerves raw. The summer I married Benjamin, moved across the country, and began seminary, I awoke many nights in the midst of full-blown panic attacks, driven from sleep by my pounding heart and detailed worries: had I calculated the cost of textbooks into our budget? Would our car pass the California emissions test? Had I married the wrong man? More often than not, the calamities I expect do not come to pass, so I replace them with new ones. Time and energy that could be used constructively—for prayer, dishwashing, learning to quilt—I sacrifice to cultivate apprehension.

My anxiety skyrocketed after the birth of Juliette. I saw it coming, of course; leave it to a true worrywart to have anxiety about the likelihood of having anxiety. I didn't foresee the depth of it, however. When Juliette was born strong and beautiful after a pregnancy with no complications, I hoped a wave of relief would wash over me. And it did, but ever so briefly. No sooner had the blood and vernix been wiped from my daughter's perfect fingers did I realize that the fears and anxieties of motherhood were just beginning. No sooner had I labored over this new life did it hit me: I love her, and she could die.

I tried not to think about it. I didn't know what else to do; the thought unraveled me so quickly, I couldn't bear it. As I rocked her back to sleep in the dark morning hours, I tried to train my mind not to consider all the bad things that could happen to her. But I couldn't chase them all away, especially when the newspaper kept me abreast of so many untimely and heartbreaking deaths. When Juliette was three months old, I had to temporarily swear off the *Los Angeles Times*, as the reports of the Sichuan province earthquake reawakened my own (reasonable) concern about the odds of a so-called Big One hitting close to home. Nothing fueled my anxiety more effectively than the reminder that the ground can literally shift beneath my feet at any moment, with no notice.

***

I was driving to church on a Sunday morning. Benjamin had left early to volunteer at the weekly pancake breakfast, so Juliette was in the backseat. I'd flipped on the local public radio affiliate and was absentmindedly listening to a story that was well under way. There was some translation involved, so it took a little longer than usual to catch up. And then all of a sudden I realized what the distraught woman was being interviewed about: an unfathomably brutal attack on her young daughter. The interviewer referenced that the perpetrator had been wanted for a similar attack against a three-month-old baby.

I started hyperventilating and crying, and I slammed my hand into the radio button as quickly as I could. I tried to fake a smile at my daughter—too young to understand what we had heard, but I didn't want to scare her with my histrionics—and focused on not crashing the car. No one wants to hear about such violence; when I'm depressed and anxious, I can't cope with it. What I heard played over and over in my mind like a broken record, and to my horror, I pictured it in my mind's eye. It was horrific. I didn't want to live in a world in which such things happen. I didn't want to be human if a human being could commit such an abomination. How do people go about their lives, shopping for shoes and praying for rain and eating birthday cake, when children are intentionally wounded by sadistic adults?

I don't know how I withstood the morning, how I greeted the crowd of homeless men and women who partake of our weekly pancake breakfast, how I sang soprano in the choir, or how I rattled off announcements about the upcoming board meeting and Christian Women's Fellowship luncheon. I sure as hell don't know how I preached. The lectionary text for the week was Hebrews 5:1–10, which casts Christ in a priestly role. I'd read a wonderful commentary in *Feasting on the Word* that opened the scripture to me. The theme of the sermon was that Christ, as our high priest, lifts up a sacrifice of lamentation on behalf of all the people. He cries and weeps and prays for us, for all humanity. My voice thickened with tears at the climax of the sermon, when I alluded to the suffering in the world. It was probably effective. If you were a cynical listener, you might wonder if I had carefully manipulated my emotions to impress the congregation with the depth of my compassion. The truth is, when my voice broke, I almost lost it completely, grieving for what happened to those children. Grieving for what could happen to my child. I am terrified I am going to lose my child. I am terrified that by giving voice to that fear, I'm communicating to the universe (to God?) that I'm the consummate target to become a bereaved parent.

***

In the midst of this season of solicitude, a church member's daughter died unexpectedly. I was still a relatively new minister, having had just enough education and experience to have a basic grasp of what to say and do and, even more importantly, what *not* to say and do. The conventional wisdom is that a simple, nonanxious ministry of presence is what people in crisis need the most—just showing up and embodying the compassionate presence of Christ. Yet each week as I visited with her, my spirit disintegrated a little more as I was forced to imagine what I would feel like if I lost Juliette. It was the last thing I wanted to imagine, a selfish thought to have while praying with a grieving mother. I can't even figure out how parents survive the *possibility* of losing a child. That central mystery breaks down into a thousand anxieties: How can I even strap her into a car seat when I know the statistics of automobile fatalities? How can I trust anyone to babysit her when no one ever suspects the caregiver might be abusive? How shall I ever let her ride a bike, drive a car, or run off to some faraway state where natural disasters are a given?

How can I live—and let her live—with the reality of death? My anxiety has consequences beyond the sharp pain that often radiates between my shoulder blades and the dull ache that drums on my temples. If I can't change, Juliette will be hounded by shadows conjured by my anxiety. She'll never outgrow her childhood fears of the boogeyman if I act as though he exists. She won't be able to enjoy her life if I tether it with my fears about her death.

So I seek healing, for her sake and for mine. And while the resources of the mental health community are a part of my recovery, they are not sufficient. At the risk of reawakening old associations connecting mental illness to sin, I do experience anxiety as a soul-sickness. For me, it is a spiritual condition as much as it is a clinical prognosis. When I give in to my anxieties, I neglect the witness of scripture. I reject Christ's teaching to consider the lilies of the field. As I fear the changing of the earth, the shaking of the mountains, and the foaming of the seas, I scoff at the psalmist's promise that God is our refuge and our strength, a very present help in trouble. Anxiety has a way of turning otherwise faithful Christians into foxhole atheists. I'm too busy worrying to pray, so preoccupied with anticipatory grief that I can't even properly lament.

There is a danger, though, as I draw upon the resources of my faith tradition. For adherents of a religion founded upon the renunciation of idolatry, Christians excel at the art of making and worshipping idols, and idols are especially tantalizing to the anxious. The one that is thrust on me by well-meaning friends is the god of optimism: the god to whom you pray for absolute security. This god is supposed to keep you and yours safe. It is the god who selectively rescues people in need, the god who would never let anything bad happen to those who worship him. The problem with this god is that the moment something bad does happen to those who worship him, he is abruptly and irreversibly reduced to a pile of crumbled stone. He isn't real, not in the way the God who created the heavens and the earth is real. He doesn't breathe; he isn't in a relationship. He sits there on the shelf next to the rabbit's foot passively echoing platitudes. He is just as dead as the rabbit.

No, the faithful answer cannot be to worship a god who vandalizes the face of the unknown with a cheery array of empty promises. The God the scriptures reveal—the God who lives and breathes and loves—hems us in and caresses us with holy hands. But this God does not vow to intervene every time we stub our toe; this God does not even bar us from making our bed in hell. But we do not go into that dark night (gently or otherwise) alone. There is no place where we can extract ourselves from the presence of the Holy One. David, in a fit of something that sounds an awful lot like anxiety, swears, "Surely the darkness shall cover me, and the light around me become night" (Ps. 139:11). But even in his terror, David knows that darkness is not dark to God, and the night is as bright as the day.

This is the God upon whom I must call, the God in whom I can trust. There are moments when I would give anything to worship the idol god over the true God. There are days when a God who simply creates me and loves me and dwells with me seems like an ineffective substitute for a god who builds an impenetrable wall around my family, around my Juliette. I have to practice rejecting the lure of the idol. You can stand on the Rock, but you can't live, move, and have your being in stones.

There is something else. If fear and anxiety are about death and lead to death, well, the true God has good news. The gospel does not only give flesh and bones to the presence of God. Through Jesus Christ, our high priest who knows firsthand the vulnerability of life, death is vanquished. I know this, at least in theory: I confess and proclaim the death and resurrection of Christ. But my anxiety has taught me that believing in the risen Christ cannot be a mere intellectual exercise. God's Easter promise that life shall be restored to life eternal must inform the whole of my life. As Alyosha puts it in the redemptive culmination of *The Brothers Karamazov*, "Ah, children, ah, dear friends, do not be afraid of life. How good life is when you do something good and rightful!" We do not live in fear that death might surprise us or even live fully because we know that one day we will die. We entrust ourselves to eternity and live to the glory of God. I like how Wendell Berry says it: "Practice resurrection."

Practice resurrection. For me, this means forcing myself to be brave enough to enjoy simple pleasures with my family. I take long walks with Benjamin, pushing the stroller throughout the neighborhood and marveling at the gaudy excess of the bougainvillea. I bake honey wheat bread, listen to folk music, and tend the zucchini plants. I nurse my daughter, which is the most good and rightful thing I've ever done. I breathe. And little by little—baby steps—I invite the real God, the God of love, to banish my fear. *How good life is.*

10

Namesake

I was sixteen the last time Louise Trotter traveled the two hours from Columbus, Ohio, to visit my mother. I came home from school to find them laughing together on the back porch. Late summer sunlight filtered through the branches of the oak trees, dappling their cheeks and coffee mugs. They may well have been sitting there since lunch; their conversations were endless, one story unfolding into the next. My mother is a constitutionally cheerful woman, but when Louise came to town, her cheer expanded into joy.

Louise was the only adult I was allowed to call by first name, which somehow made her a sort of window into my mother's spirit. Louise reminded me that my mother was a person, not only a person who had a life before marriage and kids, but a person who still had a life beyond my existence. That day in the backyard, I hung out for a few moments, soaking in Louise's hearty laugh and chatting about my new English teacher—Louise had a doctorate in children's literature and was always curious about what I was reading and writing—and then I took my leave, as much to grant them the space they needed as to return to my customary role as the sullen adolescent of the house.

A couple of afternoons later, a mutual friend of theirs called to share the news. Louise had been killed in an automobile collision.

Her death shattered that window to my mother's spirit. Which isn't to say that her spirit itself was broken, though I think in losing Louise we all sustained fractures that will never fully heal. What I mean to say is that there was not so much as a pane of glass for my mother to hide behind. Her grief was raw, exposed. She wept during the funeral, soundless tears, while my father gripped her hand in his.

I tended my own anguish by making resolutions. I couldn't have known Louise and not make my life worth something. I had to fill my days with words and stories and music and laughter—the things that made her eyes sparkle. The things she shared with my mother. I didn't discern in that moment that I was called to ministry, but the oracle whispering such possibilities in my ear was magnified.

I also vowed, as I stared at the darkened stained glass fenestra, that if I ever had a daughter, her middle name would be Louise.

***

I met Lara on the first day of seminary. She approached me after class to tell me that she wrote poems, too; in our class introductions, I had self-importantly disclosed that I had just completed my first full-length poetry manuscript. I took down her phone number without any intention of dialing it, mainly because she had also referred to her passion for journaling. I was in a phase in which I thought any use of the word "journal" as a verb was dweeby and that anyone who opted for that syntax was also, by extension, a dweeb. She presented as someone who was just a hair too touchy-feely for comfort. Which is true, for sure, but years later I just roll my eyes and punch her on the arm when she tells me I should be doing daily affirmations.

Not more than a month after I'd written her off, Lara invited me to join a carload of women who were attending a sunset drum circle at Venice Beach. Not exactly my scene, but I was getting a little antsy about my lack of new friends. I was willing to come home smelling like burnt sage if that's what it took to finally connect with my fellow seminarians. The four of us ended up dancing like lunatics as the sun collapsed into the sea. We were drenched in sweat by the time we made our way to a pizza shop, and we were so hungry we didn't care the place had been branded with a "C" from the Los Angeles County Department of Public Health. Over dinner we talked nonstop. I realized I liked each of them a *lot*—Nadja, with her astonishing length of blond hair and stories about growing up in a staunchly Communist family in East Germany; Rosamond, whose posture and grace testified to her training as a classical violinist; and Lara, who spoke of her desire to make a spiritual pilgrimage to Brazil in one breath and in the next recounted uproariously funny tales of her stint as an early morning radio deejay in Pittsburgh, Pennsylvania.

There was scant light fraternization with Lara. It must have taken a week, a month even, for us to go from recent acquaintances to dearest friends, but it seems to me that it happened in an instant. Now, when I recall that first semester of my theological education, it dawns on me that as surely as I was cramming for history of Christianity examinations and wading through chapters of Calvin, I was also enrolled in an immersion class: the life of Lara. Her schedule invested as many noncredit hours in me. And with all due respect to my inimitable professors at the Claremont School of Theology, I learned at least as much about ministry and spirituality and care from conversations with my new friend as I did from all those seminary classes combined.

The summer after Lara moved a thousand miles away, we had a chance to meet for a day in Portland, where I was in town for a denominational assembly. Lara suggested we walk the labyrinth that had been laid out by the spiritual care team in one of the hotel ballrooms. People approach labyrinths differently—some pray, some meditate, and some focus on a particular issue that requires discernment. Some, myself occasionally included, try to get past the feeling that they have entered a zombie cult. Despite my struggles with boredom and self-consciousness, I love the symbolism of meandering one's way into the center, turning around, and following the same path back into the world, changed. (I have clearly been friends with Lara a long time to write a sentence like that.) As I followed her into the painted coils, our relative positions shifted. I walked behind. We walked abreast. We walked apart. We followed the structured curves of the labyrinth until we reached the center and embraced, at which point I wept. And then it was time to follow the serpentine path back into the world, where the roads don't always converge.

***

On a Sunday morning five months after Juliette was born, Lara played hooky from her denominational assembly to bless our baby. I could have handled the ritual myself. Plenty of ministers bless and baptize their own sons and daughters, but I wanted to be just the mama for a spell. I wanted Lara to bless my daughter and to consecrate our parental vows just as other ministers had consecrated our marital vows and my ordination vows. We had worked together to craft a litany of dedication to draw the whole beloved community into the covenant, and then Lara took Juliette into her arms. She spoke to her about the rainbow she'd witnessed on the day of Juliette's birth, and that's the thing about Lara. She *has* to be touchy-feely, because she really is the sort of person to whom rainbows happen on momentous occasions. So there was a bit about how rainbows are signs of God's promise and love, a charge to receive her identity as a beloved child of God, and then a simple prayer of blessing. Lara placed her hand on her brow and spoke her name: *Juliette Louise*, and I knew all at once why she had to be the one to bless my baby with the lilting, pretty name.

Though the words of grace Lara tendered that day were sweet, the deepest blessing she bestows upon little Juliette is the one she confers through years and across far too many miles: the gift of her friendship. It is a blessing that mirrors the one I received from my daughter's namesake, my mother's best friend.

Juliette will call Lara by her first name.

11

Suffering

In the memory, we are huddled in a hospital waiting room. My mother is wearing her old horn-rimmed glasses, and though the lenses make her nearsighted eyes appear smaller than they really are, they are large with worry. I think she lets out a whimper as the nurse pries me from her arms, but it's hard to hear her over my own hysterics. I am scheduled for an operation to fix the twin hernias that formed, so the story goes, because I screamed so much as a baby.

Only when this all happened, I was still a baby. I've always sworn that my oldest memory is real, but the records indicate that I was twelve months old when the surgeon caught the protrusions just before they were primed to rupture. Even if I wanted to argue that I have supernatural powers of recollection, my attention to detail betrays me: the paint specks on my mother's glasses are a hue that wasn't yet on our bathroom walls in 1981.

My false memory can't be too far afield from reality. Indeed, I think I've constructed a conceivable scene, extrapolated from a lifetime of receiving my mother's empathy. Her face is as plain as truth in my mind's eye: the look so pained it seems as though she is the one whose insides have swelled, she is the one whose knees have been bloodied against the asphalt drive. I wanted her to be in the delivery room when Juliette was born, but I had to lecture her in between contractions; her aghast expression only made labor seem that much more alarming. My sisters and I have joked that we didn't get in trouble for mischief when we were kids; go ahead and behave like a brat—just don't you *dare* injure yourself in the process.

Anyone who has subconsciously uttered his father's trademark phrase or copped that quirky mannerism of her mother has encountered the inevitability of inheritance. Sure enough my own brow contorts into an identical illustration of excessive maternal torment when Juliette suffers. My mother is my fate, and so it goes for generations.

***

Her troubles started a month before her second birthday. Juliette had endured plenty of colds in her first year of preschool germ extravaganza, but her elevated temperature and temperament clued us in that something else was developing. The pediatrician diagnosed a double ear infection. A common enough ailment, not remotely alarming when you consider all the grave medical conditions that can afflict a two-year-old (I try very, *very* hard not to consider all the grave medical conditions that can afflict a two-year-old). Our kid did not have meningitis, cancer, autism, or any other infinitely more serious affliction. That said, even a small ear infection is rather worrisome to Benjamin and me, and not just because we're overreacting hand-wringers. After years of childhood infections and surgeries, Benjamin's left eardrum ruptured, and he never regained full hearing in that ear. He was more frustrated than ever with his partial deafness after Juliette's birth. It upset him to know that he wouldn't hear her cries with his good ear pressed against the pillow, and he was perennially on alert about the health of her ears. I'd also had chronic infections throughout primary school. That the otitis didn't flare up until she was well into the toddler era was a minor miracle, considering the histories of our ears.

A standard dose of penicillin worked like the miracle it truly is. But when the fever and chills returned six weeks later, the antibiotics didn't make so much as a dent. After a couple of rounds of increasingly strong meds, we were referred to an otolaryngologist, who unsurprisingly advised surgery to insert tubes into her eardrums. It's the typical treatment for chronic pediatric ear infections; Benjamin went through it at least twice in each ear. The downside of going to the preeminent ear doctor in town was that Juliette would have to wait over three weeks for a spot on his operating calendar. I wasn't exactly eager for her to undergo general anesthesia, but at that point the infection had been beleaguering her for nearly two months.

Three more weeks of sleepless nights did not appeal. The doctor, who was a facsimile of the Swedish chef from *The Muppet Show*, shrugged, handed Benjamin a prescription slip bearing yet another illegibly scribbled and equally unpronounceable antibiotic, and loped off to peer into the next kid's ears.

The telltale symptoms reappeared the day after her pre-op appointment at the hospital. Her fever skyrocketed, and unlike the illnesses of the past that evoked impressive screaming fits, she was lethargic and quiet. We watched her ignore an episode of her favorite show—*Wow Wow Wubbzy*—while we debated whether or not to drag her into the pediatrician's office again. "She's scheduled to have the surgery on Tuesday," Benjamin argued. I fretted that they wouldn't operate if she had a high temperature. I prevailed; Juliette didn't even protest when we turned off the television before Wow Wow found his kickety kickball.

It was a Saturday, so our best option was the understaffed weekend walk-in clinic. The physician on duty was my least favorite doctor in the practice. When Juliette was six months old, he advised me to begin supplementing her diet with formula. Against the protocols of the American Pediatrics Association and without so much as a glance at roly-poly Juliette, who was in the ninetieth percentile for weight, he explained, "Most women can't support an infant on breast milk alone." That I deigned to allow him near my child again demonstrates the depth of my concern that day.

It was a mistake. The doctor decided that Juliette's ears looked just fine and that her temperature was too high to indicate otitis, anyway. He wanted to check for a urinary tract infection . . . not a simple task with a child who was not yet potty-trained. He brusquely explained that a nurse would be in to tape a bag into her diaper, the contents of which we would then plop into a sterilized cup and drop off at the lab. Easy-peasy. He departed with the promise that he would call in a prescription to the pharmacy once the test results were in.

In walked the nurse who had startled us with her bedside manner (crappy) and technique (stabby) during Juliette's two-year inoculations. Who else could we expect to see? She slapped an adhesive bag onto the most sensitive skin on Juliette's body as if she were giving a hockey player a high five. My daughter screamed. After an hour and a half of hysterics—she even cried out repeatedly throughout her afternoon nap—I was fed up. I'd been making my contorted anguished mama face so long it was threatening to stay that way. No one had warned us that this was going to be torture. I opened her diaper to discover that the sharp edge of the vinyl bag had been shoved against her skin. An ugly red line marked where it had hurt her.

We spent the evening trying to pilfer a urine sample. At one point, the most irrational thought I have ever had in my life crossed my mind: *I'll just pee in the cup* for *her*. Which, you know, works gangbusters if you're trying to help someone pass a drug test but is less effective if your objective is to smoke out a bladder infection. In this case, we couldn't get the drugs until we mustered up the pee.

It didn't work.

She awoke at midnight, sick enough to make us panic. Her flesh was burning up, and she shook so violently I wondered if she was having a seizure. "I want to sleep," she whispered pitifully, but Benjamin and I concurred that we had to take her to the emergency room, even if such excursions are always twice as lengthy and three times as expensive as one might estimate.

The sun had already risen when the emergency room doctor confirmed that Juliette's ears were severely infected and were unquestionably the reason for her sorry state.

***

Back at the hospital for the third time in a week, we recreated my false memory with resigned precision. There's no chance Juliette will retain her morning in the day surgery unit; they give kids a dose of sedative before they put them under. It all but guarantees a veneer of amnesia will protect them from the trauma. The worst part was post-op, just as we'd been warned. Children have a dreadfully hard time waking up from the anesthesia. The nurse seemed convinced that I should be the one to hold her in the rocking chair, but Benjamin rescued me after just minutes of wrangling our howling, thrashing two-year-old. We both know that he is the one with the strength for such circumstances. As he peeled her from my shoulders, which she was simultaneously gripping and pummeling, I understood that I was being released to do what I have the strength to do: suffer with my child.

***

There's an old theological conundrum: if God is both omnipotent and beneficent—all powerful and altogether good—why does the world suck as royally as it does? (OK, maybe that's not precisely how the question was presented in seminary, but you get the gist.) The orthodox answer generally points to good old free will; there's evil in the world because people sin, and God would never intervene when the sacrosanct prerogative for humans to be assholes is on the line. The line of reasoning strikes me as reminiscent of the way certain Americans venerate the Second Amendment. The right to bear arms is untouchable, regardless of how many innocent lives are snuffed out by irresponsible or violent people with access to guns. If it were up to me, we'd black out that wrong-headed right with permanent marker. And if it were up to me (and again, the world shall rejoice that it is not), I would rather just pencil a line through the bit about divine omnipotence. It is so infinitely important to me that God is good, and I just can't reconcile that a good God would stand by doing nothing while people are suffering. I imagine God getting down on God's hands and knees and weeping with those who suffer. If Jesus is any indication—and I'm fairly sure he is—God is compassionate to a fault. Empathetic all the way to the cross, fully experiencing the potential pain of having hands and feet and internal organs. Indeed, my very favorite biblical narrative is the one from the first chapter of Mark, in which Jesus' guts turn with compassion for the leper. It's often translated as if the incarnation is an embarrassment; instead of loving the man so ferociously his innards roiled, Jesus simply "felt sorry" for him. But the Greek doesn't lie. The Word doesn't stop at becoming flesh; the flesh suffers with us and for us.

Our parents are not only our fate, but our first images of the divine. Their strengths and weaknesses are as likely to form our understanding of God as anything we learn in Sunday school or, for that matter, seminary. When I think of my mother's face, contorted in empathy for my pain, I see the face of Christ. Maybe it's true that God should pull God's self together from time to time and stop all that fussing. Lord knows overreacting makes it worse. But maybe what we need, whether our crisis is large or small, is a God who gets God's spleen all up in a twist on our behalf . . . but I suppose we also need a God who is powerful enough to embrace us while we thrash.

Thank heavens I only crossed out "omnipotent" in pencil.

12

The Tacky Plastic Fish Ring

Benjamin is the fun one. I'll get on the floor and act silly from time to time, but he endures tea parties and matchbox car races on a daily basis. He's fun for Juliette because he has so much fun himself. "I'm just immature," he claims. I prefer to think he has a great capacity for delight. When Juliette learns a new trick during playtime—stacking blocks, for instance—I'm entertained for a moment, but then I promptly return to reading whatever young adult series has captured my attention for the month (for the record, yes, I have been sucked into Forks, but the literary claptrap is balanced by visits to Hogwarts, Avonlea, and the prairie). Despite my best attempts to look interested while fretting about how Laura Ingalls's family will ever survive the great Minnesota grasshopper plague, Juliette knows I'm bored. She'll catch me surreptitiously reaching for my novel during a game of checkers and implore me with a multisyllabic "Nooooo, Maaaamaaaa!" In my defense, a game of checkers with Juliette involves moving checkers around the board in no discernible pattern until it is time to play chess.

Unsurprisingly, Benjamin is also the one who whisks Juliette off to the petting zoo, the children's museum, and the ethnic festivals. I miss many of these trips because I'm preparing board reports and making hospital calls; my regular contribution is to flag them down in the driveway to nag about reapplying sunblock. Even on my Sabbath days, the prospect of carting a temperamental toddler through teeming masses of humanity doesn't sound, well . . . *fun*. Yet my friend MaryAnn says that when it comes to parenting, "The hard thing is the easier thing." She explains that "it's easier to call them First Officer Caroline and Lieutenant Margaret and Sergeant James and pretend to dodge asteroids (traffic) and dock the lunar lander in the garage than to zone out and drive and shop and chase them around with a toothbrush." Two-year-olds' games may bore me to tears, but my lazy parenting bores Juliette to inconsolable tears. I can do better.

Such was my lofty goal—to be a more fun and therefore better mother—the day I picked Juliette up from her morning at the Montessori preschool with tickets to the aquarium in the pocket of my jean skirt. Benjamin was working on his senior thesis, and he had learned from experience that it's easier to concentrate on primary documents from the McCarthy proceedings without having to tune out whiny supplications for more string cheese. On the way to Long Beach, we shared an order of french fries. (Not sure if that counts toward my better mother score. Probably not, unless Juliette is the judge.) She fell asleep just as we were about to arrive, so we parked in the lot. I read while she napped. Thankfully, we paid a flat rate for our spot. I'm as cheap as I am lazy, and I wouldn't want to pay five dollars an hour for our bonus leisure time. So far Project Fun was really working out in my favor.

Juliette revived. "I want to see the fish," she said in between gulps of water. Falling asleep with your lips encrusted with greasy french fry salt makes for a parched awakening.

Off to the fish we went, toddling around at her pace. Like every other kid since the release of a certain Disney flick, Juliette especially loved the orange clownfish. "There's a Nemo, Mama! Two Nemos!" We were both mesmerized by the sea turtles, which were so graceful and luminous I understood why they have long been imbued with spiritual significance. (Incidentally, when I went looking for more information about the symbolism of turtles, I found connotations to both motherhood and laziness. Hmmph.) We squealed when the miniature shark came charging toward our spot by the glass; even with a solid boundary between us, those teeth were frightening.

Having exhausted our attention spans for all things bright and beautiful, all creatures great and small, we headed for the door. We were just about to escape when Juliette eyed the bane of parental existence: the gift shop. How I longed to skip it. Not only did I dread the all but inevitable temper tantrum, but after seeing a leafy sea dragon in person, tawdry souvenirs are even less compelling. We moseyed through, inspecting the various and sundry pens, stuffed fish, and plastic stingrays that help pay the aquarium bills. Juliette didn't ask for anything until we found a tiny model of a sea turtle. It was cheap, and though it was neither graceful nor luminous, I thought it might remind us of the real one. Besides, she asked nicely. "Please, Mama?" I'm a pushover for *please*.

We waited in line for the cashier to check us out. A long line of weary parents and overstimulated children stood ahead of us. I was clearly not the only mother who had been dragged into the shop by a kid who was too tired to behold any more seahorses but still had boundless energy to peruse consumer goods. Just as it was our turn, Juliette encountered a display full of tacky pink plastic fish rings—sort of like miniature snow globes, except with little neon sea creatures bobbing aimlessly inside. "I want this one," she declared, slipping it onto her thumb. It was just the sort of thing that sets my eyes rolling. All those signs throughout the aquarium about conservation and boycotting plastic bags, and then this tacky jewelry destined for landfills. Or, ironically, the Great Pacific Garbage Patch, that Texas-sized mass of manmade debris floating between San Francisco and Honolulu. At least the sea turtle wasn't as tacky. It had a sort of educational aura about it, if you set the bar low enough. Even if it wasn't an accurate rendering, at least it wasn't a neon pink vertebrate. Trying to be the fun mom who does not impose her own aesthetics on her poor kid, I told her she could pick between the two, though not without some wheedling. "Don't you like the turtle better?"

"No, I like the ring," she declared, admiring the way the sea creatures floated aimlessly within their clear plastic dome.

On our way back to the car, we paused by the harbor to study the boats lined up along the docks. Just as I snapped a sweet picture of Juliette looking out to sea, the ring slipped off her finger, bounced off the heavy railing, and promptly ricocheted into the ocean.

My first thought: "I knew that piece of junk was going to end up polluting the ocean."

And my second thought: "*No way* am I buying another one."

Juliette was distraught. "My ring, Mama! Get my ring, Mama . . . please!" To her credit, she didn't wind up to a full-fledged fit, but she was pitifully sad. I had a flash of wanting to make it better. I could easily charge another three dollars to the credit card to replace the damn thing. Instead, I pulled her onto my lap and settled into a bench by the waterfront.

"It stinks that your ring fell into the water, honey. I'm sorry I can't reach it."

"My ring," she said forlornly.

"Are you sad that you lost your ring?"

"Yes. *My ring.*"

And on and on, until she was ready to leave for the parking garage, and even then, she repeated her mournful refrain. "My ring. My ring. My ring."

Ultimately, the reason I didn't replace it wasn't on account of its irredeemable tackiness. I decided in that moment that I can't always be the kind of mama to immediately fix it. I'm sure there will be times when I will. But there will also be times when I need to be the mama who commiserates with a disappointed kid. There are disappointments I can't fix even if I wanted to, and it's probably good to have some practice on tacky plastic fish rings first.

By the time we got back to the car, she had recovered enough to play with her spinning top and have a snack. I gave her a bag of whole-wheat fish crackers. "Watch out for jellyfish, OK?" Juliette cackled, throwing her head back against the car seat. "Are there any sharks in there? You better eat those fish before the sharks get to them!" In the rearview mirror, I watched one last tear drop from her cheek to the collar of her flowered sundress as her giggles swelled into a belly laugh.

I felt like such a good mother.

I think I made the right decision, though I wouldn't go so far as to argue that the alternative decision would have been wrong. Juliette's chocolate brown eyes would have lit up as she skipped to the bin to fetch her replacement tacky plastic fish ring. She would have exclaimed, *"Oh, thank you, Mama. Thank you!"*—for while my daughter doesn't always remember to say please, she has a knack for unsolicited gratitude. She would have left happy. Happier. And I'd be willing to bet our zoo membership that Benjamin would have marched right back into the shop and bought her another ring. He might have even dropped the extra buck-fifty for the sea turtle. He is, after all, the fun one.

13

Goodbye, California

On our last morning in California, I let Juliette bounce on the king-sized hotel bed while Benjamin hauled the luggage down to our rental car. To be honest, I did my fair share of bed jumping as well. We also chatted into bananas. "Ring, ring! Guess what? We're moving to Chicago!" Juliette cackled and repeated, "Shhhh-cago!" into her own breakfast. The conversation ended abruptly when she demanded I peel her telephone.

I was perhaps the slightest bit excited that our departure day had arrived. It wasn't simply relief that we were finally done with the hard work of packing up our household or eagerness to begin my new job. I was grateful to be getting out of California alive and intact—admittedly, a melodramatic disposition. But when I recall the last leg of our westward journey just three weeks after Benjamin and I married, I'm not surprised that the eight years we spent on the left coast left me rattled. As our jam-packed Ford Ranger tooled past the Las Vegas city limits, the highway narrowed and the traffic thickened. By the time we hit the California border, the vehicles sharing Interstate 15 multiplied to such a bewildering level I had to turn the keys over to Benjamin and resign myself to whimpering, hands plastered over my eyes, in the passenger seat. (He'd done the same thing in the Colorado Rockies; I jumped into the driver's seat and snaked through the mountain passes with relish.) I couldn't drum up the courage to drive on the Los Angeles county freeways for another year.

I had long fancied the idea of moving to California. I even fought with my high school boyfriend about it; our assumptions about the longevity of our relationship were so unyielding that we argued about where we would live after we were married. I lobbied for California. He protested, proclaiming that moving there would be a fundamentally unethical act, given that the land does not have nearly enough water to sustain its ridiculously titanic population. I was sympathetic to his concerns, though not enough so that I didn't immediately accept a full ride scholarship from a scrappy little seminary midway between Palm Springs and the Pacific. I had a different redheaded companion by then, one who was game for an adventure and, just as crucially, didn't wake up in the middle of the night fretting about crumbling water tables.

According to my friend Jessica, who has done hard time in the call center for a nationally known insurance company, the 909 area code has an unsavory reputation. The Urban Dictionary is quick to point out that it is universally considered the crystal meth capital of the world, and my sympathies to the fine people of Pittsburgh, which was unceremoniously dubbed the "909 of the east" by some vapid character on *The O.C.* The admissions staff at my alma mater did a bang-up job of filtering out the less fantastic aspects of life in the 909. (Not that we were ever directly affected by the ubiquitous methamphetamines—at least, we had no way of *confirming* that any of the terrible drivers we encountered were under the influence of that chemical abomination.) By flying into a regional airport after rush hour, I missed experiencing the chaos of the Los Angeles International Airport and the four freeways it takes to get from there to the seminary campus. And February is the month of the year during which the mountain ranges that line the northern edge of the Los Angeles basin are never obscured by nasty yellow smog. I strolled to the dean's office for my interview in a light sweater, transfixed by the snowy peaks that I could enjoy without the encumbrance of a parka.

I imagined we would be landing in a paradise of sorts, but the California we discovered that broiling August was not the California of my dreams and admissions tours. Some people love it just the way it is and think you're crazy to think otherwise. I think otherwise. It's the parking lot in the Joni Mitchell song; even the undeveloped acres are tainted by urban pollution. Wendell Berry writes that there are no unsacred places, just sacred places and desecrated places. *They paved the Los Angeles River.* If that doesn't qualify as a desecration, I don't know what does.

Yet I don't regret having lived there. That desert landscape—and the complicated culture that has distorted it—was the stage for so much life. I can't foreswear it. It's where we learned to be husband and wife. It's where I studied the art and craft of ministry, where my community of faith placed their hands on my head and invoked the blessing of the Holy Spirit. It's where I became a pastor, unexpectedly, since our every intention was to flee eastward after graduation. That was another sleight of hand—my regional minister slipped my ministerial profile to the search committee of a little beachside congregation before the paperwork was released to the rest of the country. They had a head start over the Midwestern churches, and did I mention the church was in Redondo *Beach*?

Still, I agonized over the decision to stay. "We'll give it five years," we told ourselves. And we did just that, or close enough. My tenure at South Bay Christian Church was four years, eleven months, and one week. I never made any promises to stick around forever, but neither did I let on that the days of our lives together were like sands through the hourglass. I was melancholy during our last Christmas Eve service. That's exactly how I thought of it: our last Christmas Eve service, as if our ministry together had been diagnosed with a terminal illness. I was in the midst of increasingly serious conversations with a congregation in Illinois. The whole process felt sneaky. Adulterous. But Illinois—suburban Chicago—presented itself to us as the ideal place to resettle. A metropolis replete with deciduous trees, just near and far enough from our area codes of origin, and two-thirds of a continent from the sprawling conurbation we longed to escape. Yes, there would still be far too many cars on the road, and it was definitely a cauldron-to-fire transition as far as state governance goes.

When the chair of the search committee called me in February to officially invite me to become their new associate minister, I copped a demure attitude. It seemed like the conventional move for such conversations. "I guess I'll speak with Benjamin and call you tomorrow. . . ." But the poet Rumi teaches one should "say *yes* quickly / if you know, if you've known it / from before the beginning of the universe." I glanced at my husband. He was grinning and nodding his head. Perhaps we hadn't known it since before the beginning of the universe, but we'd known it at least since before the beginning of October. I scrapped my tempered facade and said yes quickly, though not without profound grief. There's no love lost between California and me, but some fine souls inhabit that state. A handful of them worship at 128 North Broadway in Redondo Beach. I loved being their minister so much I broke down on the Lenten Sabbath I finally confessed we were leaving. I believe what I did is technically called *ugly cry*. I couldn't read the letter I'd painstakingly crafted. "The Midwest," I hiccoughed, as if that explained everything. "We'll be closer to our family . . . I'm sorry." You don't stop being someone's sister, you don't formally dissolve the bond between friends. But one day I was their pastor, and the next, I was not.

Granted, that day found me jumping on a bed with my daughter. Quitting California was a complicated enterprise.

For weeks after we landed in Western Springs, a charming little village on the commuter rail line, I walked around in a delighted daze. Well, delight gets partial credit; the humidity factored into my stupefaction. I was nostalgic about everything from lightning to lightning bugs, and I reveled at the endless shades of green. Los Angeles might have gads of bougainvillea and oleander blooming every which way, but the Midwest makes an art form out of photosynthesis. One afternoon, Juliette woke up from her nap drenched in sweat. She never perspired in temperate Southern California, but her second-floor room was stuffy even with the breeze yawning through the open windows. She was bewildered, unaccustomed to the heft of the air. I carried her outside on my hip and brought her to the shade of an elm tree. "This is pachysandra, Juliette. We had it in my front yard when I was your age." I hadn't realized how much it mattered to me for my daughter to grow up with the same ground covering. Such a commonplace detail, but it has its work: preserving soil, sheltering roots. Though we were in a rental and didn't so much as plant tomatoes that year, I luxuriated in our freedom to settle down and establish roots; might they be so deep and lucky as those of that great elm.

When I was a student pastor, I chaperoned a youth group trip to Anza Borrego, a state park east of San Diego. Our caravan passed the Salton Sea and miles of eerie badlands on the way. The desert there is vast and dry as a valley of bones except for the few short weeks in the springtime when the rains come and seduce all manner of flora from the barren ground. A cruel cycle, really. The more explosive growth in that brief season of storms, the more kindling for the sun to scorch by midsummer. All I could think was *this is not my wilderness*. But the desert is the ultimate wilderness. It's where Jesus was shunted for those forty days of trials and temptations. It's where the early monastics fled to reconstruct the Christian faith beyond the grip of the Roman Empire. And so, too, it's where our family was tested, formed, broken, and healed.

And then, finally, it was time to take our leave. We'd had a perfect soundtrack for our westward drive; my sister Elizabeth burned a compilation CD called *California Songs* filled with odes to the state by such musicians as Roy Rogers, the Mamas and the Papas, and Rufus Wainwright. This time we only had to get as far as the airport, and there was only one song on my playlist: "Goodbye California" by Jolie Holland. Our suitcases stowed in the trunk, we piled into the car and buckled our seatbelts. We briefly grieved that we didn't have time for a final drive past the Pacific Ocean. Benjamin turned the ignition, and I pressed play on the stereo. We sang it at the top of our lungs as we sped past the purple jacarandas: "Goodbye, goodbye, California/ Goodbye to your waving trees/ To your succulent wind and all my friends/ Fare thee well, goodbye, so be it/ Amen/ Amen."

14

Room for the Holy Spirit

One of the unexpected lessons I learned in the early days of motherhood: Ira Glass is charming even at three in the morning. I once read an article by a woman who prayed the liturgy of the hours while breastfeeding, but I'm not nearly that religious. When I was too tired to read during the third or fourth feedings of the night, I loaded my music player with the digital archives of *This American Life*. The oddball stories kept me awake—sometimes too well. Just as Benjamin and I used to sit in the driveway to catch the end of a particularly compelling interview, I'd snuggle a sleeping Juliette until the story was over. I can't think of higher praise for a radio show than that an exhausted mother would voluntarily sacrifice even ten minutes of blessed sleep to tune in. Most of the time the themes of the show were irrelevant to my experience. That's the beauty of *This American Life*. The effervescent Mr. Glass and his team of curious geeks fan out across the country, searching back roads and basement apartments for characters you would never encounter otherwise. They commit their tales to tape, splice in some ambient music and earnest commentary, and voilà. Perfection.

That said, I was caught off guard by the chilling prologue to episode #317: *Unconditional Love*. In it, Ira Glass and his studio guest discussed the scientific experiments of one Dr. Harry Harlow. Dr. Harlow's work inspired two significant changes in the twentieth century: renewed social acceptance for maternal affection and the animal rights movement. He managed to achieve such disparate legacies by proving, with a series of torturous tests on rhesus monkeys, that babies need to be snuggled by their mothers.

Perhaps this was a *little* heavy for a new mother, nursing her daughter in the wee small hours of the morning.

In addition to leaving baby monkeys in isolation for as long as two years, Dr. Harlow also masterminded a test to determine whether the monkeys preferred food or contact. Mother monkeys forged of sharp wire provided milk, but the infants still cuddled with their ragdoll mothers, whose terry cloth breasts were dry.

The cruelty of Dr. Harlow's "love" experiments was shocking—even his colleagues and students fretted that he went too far in his clinical mistreatment of his research subjects. Yet I had an equally hard time wrapping my mind around the new knowledge that in recent history, maternal affection had been considered anathema. Many mothers were advised by their doctors to touch their infants as little as possible, lest unnecessary affection spoil them.

I pondered my child. She was still weeks away from returning my gaze, months away from laughing. She wouldn't be able to articulate the words *I love you* for almost two more years. Unlike the vast majority of my relationships, ours could not be rooted in verbal communication—at least not yet. I sang lullabies and read books and narrated the world to her, but our only overtly mutual connection was physical. There was the breastfeeding and seemingly endless holding, caressing, and kissing. I couldn't keep my hands off of her. I meditated on her tiny birthmark while she practiced her palmar grasp on my index finger. I couldn't imagine living in an era in which we were expected to keep room for the Holy Spirit between us. We were attached—and living in the era of attachment parenting. Sort of.

I liked the philosophy of attachment parenting; it jived with my moderately crunchy side. Unsurprisingly, it encourages strong physical and emotional attachments between parents and children. Contrary to the conventional midcentury wisdom obliterated by Dr. Harlow, attachment parenting gurus such as Dr. William Sears claim that children who are closely bonded to their parents develop greater emotional health and independence. That said, putting the principles of attachment parenting into practice seemed impractical, even impossible. I was definitely in favor of nursing, but I didn't want to get my hopes up about making it past Juliette's first six months. My fluctuating work schedule would make nursing-on-demand, well, demanding. And as for cosleeping . . . well, that's just downright *weird*. Unsafe—and wasteful! What was the use of putting together an adorable nursery outfitted with a brand new crib if the kid was going to end up tucked between us in the big bed? Surely, we could find and inhabit the middle ground between the extremes. Right?

***

By the time we received notice that Juliette's trendy black crib had been included in a massive safety recall, she had long since stopped sleeping in it. When she was four months old, I lost my ability to wake up throughout the night. Not even the dulcet tenor of my favorite NPR personality could sustain me. We'd tried all the tricks, from bundling her limbs in a swaddling blanket to velcroing a teddy bear that emitted artificial womb sounds to the slats of her crib. Every two or three hours she would awaken again, her untended fusses becoming unrestrained screams faster than I could stumble across the hall. We took turns trying to comfort her with milk and motion. Benjamin's shoulders had never been so brawny, thanks to the hours he carried her through the house singing lullabies.

We couldn't keep it up. And so, with a great sigh of resignation that was immediately subsumed by an even greater yawn of weariness, we started bringing her into the bed with us after her midnight wake-up call. Though we always maintained a healthy fear about the inherent dangers posed by the sheets, blankets, and most especially our body weight, we were quickly converted to the benefits of the family bed. Not only did I enjoy getting to be cozily sandwiched between my husband and my daughter, I didn't even have to sit up to nurse her. All I had to do was hike my shirt up, and she did the rest. Perfection.

Except that at nine months, she was waking up to nurse more than ever. Six, seven times on the worst nights; the proximity of her milk supply was just far too tempting. Out of desperation, for four traumatic nights we switched course and played hardball with Juliette's sleep issues. Following the directives of a sleep-training manual, we said goodnight, closed the door, and didn't open it again until morning (which got earlier and earlier, until, on the last night, "morning" was at two o'clock). While Juliette alternated between bawling and screaming, I logged on to www.askdrsears.com to reread my attachment parenting propaganda, ensuring that I would feel as horrible as possible about our decision:

> Science tells us that when babies cry alone and unattended, they experience panic and anxiety. Their bodies and brains are flooded with adrenaline and cortisol stress hormones. Science has also found that when developing brain tissue is exposed to these hormones for prolonged periods these nerves won't form connections to other nerves and will degenerate. Is it therefore possible that infants who endure many nights or weeks of crying-it-out alone are actually suffering harmful neurologic effects that may have permanent implications on the development of sections of their brain?

I love that "science" is suddenly a monolithic entity who "tells" us things. Reproachfully. I felt about as loving as a wrought iron monkey. At least the monkey mama gave her hungry kid milk when he asked for it.

Those hours of screaming and the cortisol they sent storming through Juliette's brain were all for naught. We called it quits after discovering that Juliette had scraped her nose raw on the netting of the travel crib in my church study. (The only thing worse than attempting to sleep train your child in the comfort of your own home is attempting to sleep train your child at your place of work.) We'd mistaken her elevated fury and panic for part of the program and let it continue for forty-five minutes into her scheduled naptime.

I've never despised myself so much as when I lifted my screeching, bleeding baby into my arms—and from the clutches of a parenting philosophy that just didn't work for our family. I promised Juliette I would never do that again, even if it meant that we would continue to cosleep until kingdom come. Or kindergarten; whatever comes first.

Maybe if we had known that Juliette would still be nursing throughout the night an entire *year* later, we wouldn't have given up so easily. Actually, if we had known that, I wouldn't have had a choice whether or not to persevere. I would have lost my mind altogether.

***

Contrary to the adage that warns it's time to stop breastfeeding when they're old enough to ask for it, I delighted in Juliette's expanded ability to communicate her needs. The first baby sign language trick we taught her was for milk, despite my reservations with its particulars—to perform the sign, one mimes the process of milking a cow. Juliette immediately adapted it into something more like the hand motion indicating money, her thumb circling the tips of her tiny fingers. Once, when Benjamin was serving as the lay worship leader in church, Juliette refused to be handed over to one of her many honorary church grandmothers. We took turns holding her: I while he led the opening prayers, Benjamin while I preached. My cheeks burned with the conviction that the members of the congregation were unusually unified in spirit, all thinking the same thought: *that is one spoiled child.* (I was mistaken; if anyone was thinking that, it wasn't universal. The first person to speak to me after worship, an eighty-year-old man, gripped my shoulders and said, "Katherine, we love her, and everything is OK.") As embarrassed as I was, I could hardly contain my snickering when Juliette, slung on her father's narrow hip, started making the universal money sign as he issued the call for tithes and offerings.

When someone innocently asked what that was all about (surely we hadn't trained our daughter to beg for money, right?), I hesitated to explain. Juliette was just short of twelve months at the time; even the not-so-crunchy American Academy of Pediatrics recommends nursing for at least a year. An older congregation, many of the members of the church had raised their kids long before the onset of the attachment parenting trend. The only time I ever breastfed Juliette in public around church members—on a retreat, out of necessity, for I do *not* nurse in the presence of toilets—I'd secreted the deed behind a bolt of cloth aptly branded a Hooter Hider. But they didn't even need to see me breastfeeding a not-so-newborn baby to be eked out that I was doing it. Not that I broadcast it, but it occasionally came up. At one point during that first year, in conversation with some trusted church leaders, I mentioned that I would need a moment between worship and a potluck to nurse Juliette. I didn't think anything of it. Soon after, a kindly older member stopped me outside the church library. "Just how long are you going to keep breastfeeding?" she asked. Caught off guard, I stammered something about our pediatrician's advice. I couldn't find the words to say what I really meant: until we're done, and I don't yet know when that will be, and perhaps it's not your business.

I loved nursing. I loved that my milk, and my milk alone, nourished her well into the ninetieth percentile for weight. I loved that she giggled and bounced with excitement when we headed to the rocking chair, that her small hand crept up to tangle my hair as she suckled. I loved the excuse to do nothing but sit there (despite a friend's prediction that I wouldn't have time to read anymore, I read fifty books before Juliette's first birthday). I feared how our relationship would change after she was weaned; for so long, the milk was just short of everything. Barbara Brown Taylor observed the loveliness of nursing in the life of her goddaughter, Madeline:

> Just three months old, she lived her life in her mother's arms, comforted by the familiar sounds and smells of the one-person universe into which she had been born. She slept, she woke, she fed at her mother's breast, finding everything she needed in that one nourishing embrace. Watching her nurse one day, I saw that her mother was truly her food, the body and blood from which her own flesh had been made and from which she daily accepted her life as a matter of course.

Nursing was sacred at three months and still would be sacred at three years, if that's how long it took for Juliette to be ready to give it up.

That said, just because something is sacred doesn't necessarily mean that it is always pleasant. I didn't love the excessive nighttime nursing, the semipermanent teeth marks on my nipples, or her stubborn refusal to drink the bottles I fastidiously pumped (even as I privately congratulated myself that silicone nipples couldn't compete with the real thing). My frustration with the nighttime nursing exploded when she was eighteen months old. I'd spent a week out of town and came home believing the era was over; instead, she wanted to nurse more than ever and screamed hysterically when I tried to withhold the milk. When it began to seem that I was serving our toddler a nightly cocktail of milk and resentment, we started making her nurse in a chair—not just before bed, as usual, but each time throughout the night that she wanted to partake. I confess that I chuckled the first time she dragged herself out of bed and across the room, exhausted. She looked how I felt. That trick alone reduced the number of feedings. After a week, we took the chair out of the room and warned her that from now on, she could nurse once before bedtime and no more. There were tears, but not as many as I expected. Words were our salvation; she understood our explanations. We still let her come into our bedroom when she awoke in the night; she nestled under the crook of my arm until morning. I found I once again took pleasure in the warmth of her breath on my cheek, asking for nothing more than to be safe and near—and I once again loved our bedtime nursing session, during which she drank milk free of maternal bitterness.

And then, one night in her twenty-fifth month, Juliette wandered into her room at bedtime and marched straight to the twin bed, where we read books, instead of the rocking chair, where we nursed. I followed her lead, not offering what she had not asked for. The next night was the same, and the night after that, and the night after that. It was finished.

Several months later I asked Juliette if she remembered "mama milk." She furrowed her brow and pointed to my chest. "I have some?"

"No, sweetheart. Mama milk is done. Would you like for me to read a book to you?" She nodded, climbed into my lap, and rested her hand on my cheek. "I love you, Juliette."

"Love you too, Mama."

Perfection.

15

Faith Development of a Two-Year-Old

"Yes, Jesus loves me, the Bible tells me so." I had intended the song to be a lullaby, but Juliette perked up when I started singing. Though I had never sung it to her before, she seemed to know it well. She sang along in her indecipherable, off-key, yet altogether adorable manner.

"Do you sing 'Jesus Loves Me' in Sunday school?" I asked.

"Yeah," she answered, nodding enthusiastically.

In the interest of my daughter's faith formation, I jumped at the chance to engage in some meaty yet two-year-old-appropriate theological conversation. "So you know that Jesus loves you."

She looked thoughtful for a moment. I waited for the brilliant spiritual insight to spring from the mouth of my babe. Instead, she smacked her rear end and giggled. "That's my butt."

Despite the irresistible distraction of heinie identification during bedtime catechism, Juliette is a fairly religious little girl. At least, there are a lot of churchy people, places, and things in her life, and she takes to them all with gusto. Born hundreds of miles from her nearest blood relative, she readily accepts church folks as stand-ins for kith and kin. As one of two toddlers in a tiny congregation, she captivated the attention of all those extra aunties and uncles and, just as they considered her "their" baby, she claimed them as her own. One of the first names she picked up, aside from Mama and Dada, was the church treasurer's; to Juliette, he was "My Don!" And he was. Marvelous with kids though he'd never had his own, Don was a substitute grandpa par excellence. He was even born in the same Chicago suburb as my father, during the same year. There were frustrations in being a young family in a small congregation composed of older members, but the warmth, love, and seemingly endless supply of homemade baby blankets Juliette received from her first church home eclipsed its lack of playmates, programs, and a child-proofed place to roam.

My father and Juliette's Don turned seventy the summer we moved to a suburb just a few train stops from their hometown. Our new church is more than twenty times larger than the congregation I served in California. There was a bouncy house at the first fellowship event we attended. Even as I watched Juliette have the time of her life—protected from the boisterous big kids by a newly adopted older "church sister"—I couldn't help but wonder if we sold out for a bouncy house. But there is a great deal more to our new community of faith than that. The First Congregational Church of Western Springs has quickly become the central location in Juliette's life. She's there several times a week for Sunday school and preschool, and the Christian education director recently nominated her to be the official reviewer for any new *Veggie Tales* movies that come in to the well-stocked church library; she hangs out in my study with Larry the Cucumber after preschool. When we're leaving the house, she asks, "Are we going to church?" and occasionally pitches a fit if the answer is no. Church has been, and I hope always will be, a sanctuary for my daughter.

We don't have to leave the house for some aspects of her spiritual formation. Reading has always been crucial to my faith (where would I be without my tattered copy of *Traveling Mercies*?), so it's no great surprise that I'm a hopeless sucker for children's books that master the rare combination of solid theology and beautiful art. We own most of the good ones. I rejoiced the day Juliette pulled *Big Momma Makes the World* by Phyllis Root from her bookshelf, asked me to read it, and sat through the whole thing. I may have shed an actual tear when she implored, "Again!" The only thing that could make me happier than reading a feminist retelling of the Judeo-Christian creation story to my toddler is fulfilling her request to read it again. I didn't even remind her to say please. Despite my best intentions to keep the schlock out of her religious book consumption, a growing girl has opinions. For weeks she was mildly obsessed with a toddler Bible she insisted we check out from the church library. It was not the toddler Bible I would have selected, with the tasteful pictures and richer language. This one was illustrated cartoonishly, with a blond Jesus and disciples who, despite looking like they were three years old, sported handlebar mustaches. Theologically, it was harmless, so I figured I could forgive her questionable aesthetics. Besides, in the midst of her book obsession, I brought her to a Christmas carol sing-a-long. When the band started singing about the little Lord Jesus making no crying sounds (*yeah right*), she started jumping up and down. "Jesus?" she exclaimed, beside herself with excitement. "I have that book!"

Now that Juliette is more verbal and aware, we've finally gotten into the habit of praying together before meals. (Busted. Despite my good intentions, I've never been much of a grace-sayer.) My own family always sang Johnny Appleseed before meals. I know Juliette would love that, but I haven't introduced it because I also want her to learn to use words to thank God for her blessings. For several weeks, when it was Juliette's turn to pray, I would prompt her and she would repeat the prayer back. But the other night, she took charge. "Dear God, thank you for . . ." In the pause, I dreaded that we might be in for another butt reference. "Everything! Amen."

Out of the mouths of babes and infants, indeed.

Surely, Juliette's spiritual life—her life in general—will be shaped in part by my ministerial vocation. Not having sprung from the loins of preachers myself, I'm not intimately familiar with the vicissitudes of life as a preacher's kid. I hear there are pitfalls to the position. Everyone assumes you will behave because you are the preacher's kid or assumes you will *not* behave because you are the preacher's kid. You can't win either way. I've wondered what Juliette thinks when she sees me during coffee hour (read: doughnuts and far-too-many-cups-of-lemonade hour) in my clerical robe and liturgical stole, in the midst of all the people in street clothes. Perhaps it is a sight she has seen so often and from such an early age it doesn't register. But at some point, she may wonder why I am set apart from all but my clergy colleagues. I learned painfully quickly that ordination didn't make me a better wife or friend or daughter; neither does it make me a better mother.

Still, the same fascination with all things spiritual that pulled me into ministry pushes me to take an active role in guiding Juliette's emerging spirituality. I'm not especially confident about my capacity to do this well. My own spiritual life tends to comprise equal parts faith and doubt. I love Jesus but treasure nuance; the day I learned that there can be a difference between truth and fact was the closest I've ever come to a genuine conversion experience. Though my theological education barely brushed on the spiritual development of children, I'm certain that such fine distinctions would be lost on my daughter. Her interest in the number of angels dancing on the head of the pin ends the moment she realizes they are not ballerina princesses. I don't want to dismiss my theological education entirely. It's as relevant to my parenting as it has been to my ministry in general, which is to say, sort of, and probably most often in retrospect.

I don't have a trove of childhood experiences to fall back on; although we were regular attenders of a relatively conservative United Methodist Church, my parents did not talk about matters of faith. Several years ago, I asked my father about the lack of Godtalk in our household, and he looked uncomfortable as he explained that religion is a private matter. (He gets the same pained expression on his face when I press him to discuss politics.) I think they figured the trained experts—that is, the volunteer Sunday school teachers— would fill in the blanks. I can't do that. Not because I don't trust the Sunday school teachers but because I am convinced that relegating spirituality to church and church alone is the best way to render the whole business irrelevant. Family is such a primary resource for who we are as human beings; to cut Christ out of the family portrait is terribly sad to me as someone who tries, for better or for worse, to be one of his disciples.

I'm charmed by the concept of the family as a "little church." St. John Chrysostom coined the term, Martin Luther revived it by renouncing his vows of chastity and getting himself a wife and several progeny, and many a Catholic pope has infallibly decreed it. With so much traction in the Church universal, the "little church" movement is rife with moderately icky aspects. Much of the literature and tradition related to the concept assumes that the man is necessarily the spiritual head of the household. But like a whole host of Christian traditions, this one is worth reclaiming as well and is easily reframed in egalitarian terms. Our first formal attempt at maintaining a family liturgy was quite lovely; thanks to the Christian education committee at the First Congregational Church, we started Juliette's third Advent season equipped with a homemade wreath and family-friendly devotionals. Juliette loved the ritual of gathering around the table after supper to light candles, hear a story, sing a song, and say a prayer. Her favorite part was blowing the candles out—my least favorite part, as I do not care to have my baby anywhere near open flames.

I was melancholic when I dismantled the wreath on Epiphany day. I liked our "little church" service, and while we could certainly come up with something else to do during the long string of ordinary days between the seasons of Epiphany and Lent, I missed the tangibility of the wreath in our midst. But then it hit me: *communion*. I am ordained in the Christian Church (Disciples of Christ), a tradition that celebrates communion weekly. I didn't always love the ritual, but several years of consecrating the elements every Sunday morning has made me hungry for the bread and cup. My present congregation is affiliated with the United Church of Christ, which only partakes on the first Sunday of each month. My belly growls for spiritual food by the time the fourth Sunday of the month rolls around. But Disciples have an unusual take on communion. They don't put any fences around the Lord's table; laity can preside, and so long as everyone who is present is welcome to participate, there's no law against blessing bread and juice at home. A quick trip to the grocery store for grape juice and we had everything we needed to continue the liturgical portion of our little church.

This is one aspect of my daughter's young faith formation that is intentionally different from my own. One of my earliest memories of being in church was not being allowed to participate in communion. Juliette will not remember a time before she was communing with Christ and his Church. The first bread she ever tasted was King's Hawaiian sweet bread that I had blessed and broken at the marble table at South Bay Christian Church. *Taste and see that the Lord is good.* So good that when she got a little older, and discovered the deliciousness that is Welch's grape juice, it became difficult for Benjamin to bring her to worship services. She couldn't make it through the prelude without whining for the bread and juice. I suppose one could argue that's a sign she's too young to partake, but I don't subscribe to the philosophy that you have to understand the meaning of communion to receive the gift of communion. To me, the table is about hospitality. Excluding kids—excluding anyone—would be far more troublesome than zeal for grape juice. As far as Juliette can tell, communion is a snack for everyone. And on one level, that's exactly what it is.

And on so many levels, communion symbolizes everything I love most about my faith and the faith I long to cultivate in my daughter. It is a ritual that begins with a reading from a sacred book, a ritual that, even when seemingly limited to just our own family, in truth connects us to the whole Christian family. It is a ritual that reminds us that God is capable of transforming a catastrophe into a miracle. And it is a ritual with such delicious elements my daughter hungers to taste and see the goodness of God.

16

Dirty Windows and Homemade Bread

I maintain a short list of books that have changed my life. Books must present a persuasive argument to be included, and there's no accounting for quality. The first volume of *The Babysitters Club* series tops the list, because it was the first chapter book I read, and it was sufficiently compelling to turn me into a lifelong reader. The Holy Bible makes the cut, though I'll be the first to admit that it hasn't changed my life quite enough yet. I scribbled the most recent addition onto the list before it really had an opportunity to prove its transformative hold over me, I was so utterly convinced that things would never be the same: *Animal, Vegetable, Miracle* by Barbara Kingsolver. I bought the paperback at the Cleveland airport as a consolation prize for having to say good-bye to my sisters. It's a food diary, farm journal, and memoir, all focused on the year her family ate (almost) entirely locally. Toward the end of the book, she addresses the difficulty in leading people to recognize the gravity of global warming without overwhelming them to the point of deciding that it's too far gone and nothing they can do matters anyway. She aims to create a narrow clearing of hope between cynicism and apathy.

The book inspired me to request tomato plants for my first Mother's Day—a gift that is, according to Kingsolver, a tradition in Southern Appalachia. Eating locally is easy enough to do in Southern California; we could go to a farmer's market any day of the week (that said, much of California's water system is imported, so hardly anything is truly local). What I was really after was the challenge of actually doing something myself. We're sold so much convenience these days, from fast food to disposable diapers to prebaked, presliced loaves of bread. While reading *Animal, Vegetable, Miracle*, I remembered the advice John Ortberg passed along from one of his spiritual mentors in an essay in *Leadership Journal*: "You must ruthlessly eliminate hurry from your life . . . Hurry is the great enemy of spiritual life in our day." While there are certain conveniences—certain luxuries—I cling to happily, I do wonder if I'm missing out on something important by turning over so many essentials to the professionals. Perhaps saving time robs time of its sanctity.

In the years before Juliette was born, Benjamin and I were a typical child-free couple. Thanks in large part to a combination of student loans and haphazard savings habits, we had enough money to eat out several times a week. I purchased and promptly forgot about bushels worth of produce; it would have been simpler to toss the bags directly in the trash after returning from the market and spare our refrigerator the stench and mess of rotted cucumbers. When I did prepare meals, most everything came from cans and boxes. (I find it a little humorous that my contribution of cooking dinner—popping a frozen pot pie in the microwave—excused me from dishwashing responsibilities.) I did bake, though dangerously rarely. I once set out to make a rare second batch of Christmas cookies only to discover tiny weevils crawling around in the all-purpose flour. If only I'd noticed them before devouring—and worse, *distributing*—the prior batch. I also followed a strict bread-baking schedule: once a year, around the time the smudged ink date on the yeast envelope was about to expire, I mixed and kneaded and baked a loaf of country white bread. It never turned out properly, hence the year I needed to forget the unfavorable ratio of work to pleasure before I was ready to rip open another package of Fleischmann's Rapid Rise. Meanwhile, during their year of eating locally, the Kingsolver family baked all their own bread using a bread machine. They didn't consume a single loaf that had been infused with preservatives, baked in a factory, sent through an automated slicing machine, wrapped in plastic, and delivered by diesel truck to the neighborhood Super Target. They spent a few minutes every other day or so tossing a handful of ingredients into that contraption most people store in the darkest recesses of their basements. What seduced me most was the idea of living in a place blessed with the scent of freshly baked bread (which is, to my imagination, the perfume of heaven).

I started trolling Craigslist for bread machines (it's amazing how many people are desperate to offload barely used ones—enough to make you think twice before giving one as a wedding gift, even if the thing is listed on the couple's registry). But as I daydreamed about the scent of olive-rosemary bread radiating from the kitchen and nervously tended my container garden, I never managed to keep up with my share of the household chores. Baking bread, even with the assistance of a motorized appliance, is romantic and fun. Finally getting around to cleaning those windows? Not so much. I tried to convince myself that I should spruce up my housekeeping skills before investing in the twenty-pound bag of whole-wheat flour. But the still, small voice within me was positively hollering different advice. Locating that narrow clearing of hope in the midst of all that there is to fear in this world surely must require regular servings of joy. I knew that if I could just keep those tomatoes alive until August, they would not just be another humdrum afterthought to toss in the salad. They would be *my* tomatoes that I grew *myself* in collaboration with *sun* and *water* and *soil*. It would be a reason for celebration.

I don't want to waste all my time by saving it. That isn't the life I want, and that isn't the life I want for Juliette. I want to ruthlessly eliminate hurry and selectively replace convenience with joy.

And so, during one of the most trying seasons of my life, with a baby on my hip and a marriage in crisis, I intentionally started making things harder for myself. I found myself undertaking projects I'd previously considered to be Martha Stewart bullshit (not to put too fine a point on it). I pureed homemade baby food, started collecting fabric scraps to sew a sundress for Juliette, and convinced Benjamin we should invest in cloth diapers. And, in my new-to-me Williams Sonoma bread machine, I baked loaf after aromatic loaf of increasingly delicious bread.

As for the windows, they were filthy until a church member came to the parsonage for book group, took note of their condition, and out of mercy for the overly busy working mom, arranged for professionals to come by with ladders and squeegees.

***

There is a huge resurgence of interest in and respect for the arts of homemaking. The mommy-blogging world is replete with posts about cooking, baking, and gardening with little ones underfoot. And then there's the craft hobby explosion, wherein frazzled mothers work subversive embroidery designs and meticulously document their kids' childhoods in artful scrapbooks. None of it is new. Even my own mother, who raised kids in the shadow of the feminist movement, crafted Christmas ornaments out of polyester felt and, for a brief era in the late 1970s, clothed her family in garments sewn from Stretch & Sew patterns. The do-it-yourself trend presents a compelling combination of creativity, self-sufficiency, environmental consciousness, and economics. Well, sometimes economics. Certain hobbies are far more expensive than others; during the height of my knitting obsession, I appeared to be converting our savings into natural fibers.

For me, the desire to incorporate creativity into our domestic life was a source of joy—it was a happy day when I realized I could set the timer on my fancy bread machine, thereby enabling us to wake up to the smell of freshly baked bread—but the joy was dogged by persistent frustrations. I wanted to feed Juliette good, healthy, homemade food—and that wasn't an easy task after a full day's work. Benjamin fulfilled his share of the household upkeep. Not only did he change far more diapers than I did, but he was also the appointed launderer, a chore that was somewhat more involved thanks to the stinking pile of diapers that accumulated in the bathroom hamper every few days. Still, his idea of a hobby is watching sports, not learning how to preserve fresh Roma tomatoes for midwinter marinara suppers. If anyone in our little family was going to reclaim the traditional "womanly arts," it would be me. Kingsolver notes the hidden significance of those Mother's Day seedlings: "Right behind planting come the weeding, mulching, vigilance for bugs and birds, worry over too much rain or not enough. [Gardening] so resembles the never-ending work and attention of parenting, it seems right that it should all begin on Mother's Day."

Being a working parent who resists the temptation to let Kraft prepare all her family's meals is a tough road to walk without walking far too hurriedly. The funny thing is that by bypassing the "convenience" options, you sort of lose the right to feed your resentment. The Wonderbread rolls its eyes and chuckles at your folly.

The Bible seems to rather like plucky women who turn housework into an art form. Granted, the Judeo-Christian scriptures don't have the best track record on gender politics, and I've been known to quibble with some of its outmoded mores. I take that stuff with a grain of salt and trust that the lot of Lot's wife will not also befall me (lest you've forgotten, she was turned into a pillar of salt for disobeying the angels' orders). The Book of Proverbs closes with an "Ode to a Capable Wife." If you wanted to, you could read it as a sexist vision of womanhood. I don't want to read it that way at all, though. Rather, I take it as a celebration of strength, beauty, and that woefully underappreciated quality of competence. The capable wife of Proverbs 31 clothes her family with handmade garments, awakens at the crack of dawn to prepare meals for her loved ones, makes her own financial decisions, runs a craft business, and feeds the poor. She's got strong arms (this is the scripture upon which I meditate when I lift weights at the gym). She's wise and kind and unafraid. She is intimidating in the way most fabulous women are; you want to be like her, and the impossibility of actually accomplishing everything she does might evoke resentment within her less capable neighbors. But so long as we all keep in mind that this is an ode—a celebration—not a challenge, a little good-hearted emulation couldn't hurt. After Jesus, the biblical character to whom I most want to be discipled is this unnamed wife. I figure what Jesus doesn't teach (how to work a cable stitch, effective meal planning, etc.), she will cover.

The happiest blessing of my neodomestication is the pleasure of sharing these things with Juliette. Inviting her to scrub her hands, tie on an apron, and stir the batter for cookies trumps even the cookies themselves. She loves to help, and increasingly, she actually does. I used to lose track of how many cups of bread flour I dumped into the machine (sleep deprivation taxes my ability to count to three). Now we count together. She paints oil onto slices of organic eggplant, rinses unbreakable dishes, and, when prodded seven or eight times, helps tidy her toys. I'm aiming to teach her how to knit when she's five. Her growing skills please her even more than they please me. It feels good to be competent, to approach a task with ability, confidence, and grace. She sees the work of her hands and recognizes that she's making a contribution, that her presence and participation make our home a lovelier place. It's enough to make me want to write a little ode to my capable daughter. Not because she's a girl, and girls should know these things, or that one day she'll be a wife, and cooking and cleaning will be her job. But because home matters. Surrounding ourselves with beautiful and useful things, taking on beautiful and useful work, always and ever avoiding the nefarious task of window washing.

We have to leave *something* for Benjamin to do while we knit.

17

Maybe One

It took me over an hour to unwrap the gifts at the baby shower my congregation hosted for us. By the time I had gushed over the last designer burp cloth, we had filled three large trash bags with paper, tape, ribbons, and empty boxes. Later, after we transported the loot home in two tightly packed cars, we piled it up in the empty nursery. It looked as if we had ransacked the inventory of a baby boutique. There was still another layer of packaging to contend with: tags, plastic cartons, twisty ties, little boxes that had been nestled in big boxes. I awkwardly lowered myself to the ground for a second round, but I hoisted myself right back up again when I realized I needed to fetch fingernail scissors to separate countless coordinated layettes for the laundry. The second round of unwrapping took yet another hour and generated yet another jumble of refuse to be sorted for trash and recycling.

Our daughter's carbon footprint was already astonishing, and she was still weeks away from being born. Months away from establishing her long and messy dependency on diapers, which would exponentially multiply her mark on the earth. We planned to use cloth diapers and wipes as much as possible, but knew the energy and water usage counterbalanced what little landfill space we spared by eschewing disposables. If each of the more than six billion members of the human population strains the earth's resources as much as our environmentally minded family does, we're in serious trouble.

Before Juliette even emerged, I started to think: *maybe one*. Maybe this baby will be our only child. What better way to curtail someone's carbon footprint than to simply prevent his or her footprint from ever forming? I casually mentioned to a friend that the population crisis was a factor in our discernment process and quickly realized this is not the kind of thing you can mention casually. Perhaps not even at all. The implications are just too sensitive. I would never imply that second or third (or fourth or fifth) children shouldn't exist. I'm a third kid, and I'm generally pretty grateful that I was invited to the party. It's just that the global population is unsustainable. I worry about my great-grandchildren, what kind of world they'll inherit. One of the ways to address the situation is for people to start volunteering to bear less fruit.

Once Juliette was on the scene, concern for the earth became only one dimension of the case for having a small family. I didn't know if I could hack being pregnant a second time, and the thought of experiencing childbirth again gave me phantom back labor pains. Anything other than our comfortable two-to-one ratio of adults to child made us nervous, especially given our parenting style. More often than not, if one of us could do the job, we both showed up. For the first two years of her life, Juliette rarely had a bath not administered by both her mother and her father. We tag-teamed the bedtime routine, responded to minor scrapes and bruises in tandem, and usually filed into the pediatrician's office together. We also wondered if we had the emotional resources to parent more than one kid. When Juliette was of the age many parents start considering a second child, our marriage was stronger than ever. Still, we fretted that inviting such a significant change into our lives would send us back into chaos. And financially—well, let's just say that ministers don't generally make loads of cash, and Benjamin didn't exactly bring home the Benjamins when his primary vocation was staying at home with Juliette. Even with the benefit of decent health insurance, our out-of-pocket prenatal and hospital expenses were astronomical. On the bright side, though, the figure seemed like a bargain compared to the preschool bills we would eventually receive.

Ultimately, a book sent the pendulum to a sturdy "no" on further conception. Not *Maybe One*, Bill McKibben's impassioned apologetic for small families, though I did read it appreciatively. Juliette plucked the book that promised to settle the question from the travel section of our local bookstore: *Fodor's Around Paris with Kids.* Yes, the title assumes you would be toting along more than one, but as I called Benjamin over to marvel at Juliette's selection, our eyes gleamed as we concurred that we could probably swing a trip to Europe with, say, a singular five-year-old. We had spent ten days tracing Rick Steves's footsteps through western Europe shortly before I got pregnant and always hoped to return. I could already envision myself framing a photograph of Juliette, in a red beret, posing in front of the Eiffel Tower.

The power of that imagined Europe trip was less about the romance of travel (or, for that matter, the unbearable cuteness of dressing Juliette in a beret.) What struck me was the notion of our family going off on a big adventure together. In my mind's eye, I saw just that: *our family.* Complete. Instead of just considering arguments against another child—the environmental, relational, and financial strain of expanding our family—I began to see the beauty of stopping while we were ahead: Juliette Louise Pershey was and is *enough*, in the most beautiful sense of the word. If three was sufficient to round out the Triune God and the Roman triumvirate, three was sufficient for the Pershey family.

It wasn't a fortnight later that I unexpectedly burst into tears during a childbirth scene in a movie I had already watched three times before. I didn't comprehend why I was crying until I overheard myself confessing to Benjamin, "I want another baby." He talked me down, reminding me that while he was in no way ready to consider having another baby anytime soon, none of our necessary organs had been snipped or tied. We hadn't even offloaded the baby gear yet, having lugged it from California to Illinois in case the pendulum swung back to babymaking. Just because we were contracepting now didn't mean we had to contracept forever. As quickly as I'd made a beret-inspired conclusion, I forced the pendulum back to the safety zone of "maybe, but not yet" with all my might.

***

Our first autumn in Illinois was exemplary: brilliant and crisp and as colorful as a new box of crayons. Growing up in the Midwest, I'd always taken the changing leaves for granted, even dreading the onset of fall on account of the bitter cold and darkness that stalked the calendar at the beginning of November. We were finally settling into our altogether different life. Benjamin had been hired by a nonprofit on the North Side of Chicago, helping recently homeless women gain housing and employment stability. His return to full-time work was a significantly harder transition for our family than even moving across the country; Juliette and I were used to him being around and now his long work days began and ended with a thirty-mile commute. Juliette attended school almost full time. On alternate mornings, she joined me at church, playing for a couple of hours with her friends in the preschool program and hanging out afterward in my study eating string cheese and drawing on my recycled sermon manuscripts. Mornings were less peaceful as Juliette and I struggled to get out of the house on time, and the predinner witching hour was trickier without another parent to share the burden of Juliette's five-o'clock crankiness. Still, the new arrangements were tolerable and I looked forward to the possibility that we might be free of major life changes for a spell.

And then one morning, Juliette rolled over in bed and said, all matter-of-fact, "Mama, there's a baby in your belly."

I'm not the ghost-conjuring, psychic-telephoning, tarot card–reading type, but I reluctantly believe in ESP. All the women in my family have experienced randomly occurring instances of just *knowing* something. For me, it's never been anything weighty. Every seven years or so I know beyond a shadow of a doubt that I will win a raffle or door prize, and I've never been wrong yet. Benjamin has his own extrasensory perception, but it's both oblique and scattershot. A recent dream about the R&B artist Seal turned out to be unexceptional (by all accounts, Seal is alive and well), but I still shiver when I think about the dream he had the night before Johnny Cash died. He told me about it at dawn while we were still spooned under the bedspread. He and Johnny had been together on a sound stage. Benjamin was jamming on the country legend's guitar (the aspect of the dream that is most bizarre, considering Benjamin's lack of musical skill). Johnny ambled over, leaned down to give him a kiss on the forehead, and walked away.

So Johnny Cash bid farewell to my husband before finally responding to his mother's voice beckoning him home for suppertime, and I knew that I was going to win the salon gift certificate in the silent auction at my senior prom. That doesn't mean my kid has some sort of supernatural early pregnancy–detection gene. Right? I told myself she must have been around a lot of expecting mothers at church, or maybe she had heard us celebrating her Aunt Marie's pregnancy. Just because I was increasingly nauseated and achy and hungry and thirsty didn't mean *anything*, and certainly the fact that I'd gone off the pill a few weeks ago but hadn't gotten around to taking my new diaphragm out of the box was *completely irrelevant*. There's a grace period for conception, right? No? Surely, there had to be a reasonable explanation. The seasons were changing! I was reacting to the cold! I had premenstrual syndrome! I held off on buying a pregnancy test for a week. I might have actually bought one sooner had Juliette not made her proclamation. It was far too weird to imagine that she might actually be right.

She was actually right.

When we told her the news, she wasn't remotely surprised. The child practically rolled her eyes. "I know, Mama."

So much for a spell without change. So much for being the noble volunteers willing to selflessly curtail our sexual reproduction for the sake of poor, beleaguered Mother Earth. So much for my selfish desire to never endure another three months of morning sickness.

So much for Paris. And I didn't care.

Correction: I still care about the environment. We'll just have to practice excellent stewardship as a family of four, even if it means that kid number two must reuse Juliette's pink car seat, regardless of her or his gender. But I chose not to be overwhelmed by the wonky timing. I chose not to worry if the senior pastor would be peeved about discussing maternity leave so soon into my tenure (he wasn't). I chose to turn down the fancy genetic screenings that had heightened my anxiety the first time around. I chose to be completely delighted with the expected blessing of carrying another child within myself.

There will be childcare arrangements to figure out, diapers to change, and more sleepless nights than we think we'll be able to survive. Benjamin and I will probably increase the regularity of our long-distance calls to our counselor in California. There will be illnesses and sibling rivalry and uncertainty. There could be another encounter with postpartum depression and anxiety; this time I hope I'll have the wherewithal to recognize it before it erupts in our faces.

I know, beyond a shadow of a doubt, that we will wonder how we could have ever imagined life without both our children. I know that we will be damn good parents to this second child, just as we are damn good parents to our beloved Juliette. At the same juncture in my first pregnancy that I was neurotic in twelve different ways before breakfast, I am uncharacteristically at peace.

Maybe one . . . *definitely* two.

18

Sabbath in Zion

Several years ago I read a book about Sabbath that scared the living daylights out of me. You wouldn't think that this could be so, but it was. A pastor wrote the book primarily for other pastors. Along with great biblical commentary, theological reflection, and wise counsel, the author, Eugene Peterson, injected enough scolding that I would shut each chapter feeling as though I had spent the last half hour in the principal's office. Which isn't to say I didn't like the book. I did. I trusted this gifted minister and writer enough to believe him when he claimed how detrimental it is when pastors—when Christians—disobey the commandment to honor the Sabbath and keep it holy. Still, when I had an opportunity to study with Peterson a couple of summers ago, I accepted the invitation with fear and trembling. I was prepared to meet a man who was stern, intimidating, and grim-faced. When I arrived at the retreat center for a week of conversations about writing and the pastoral life, I was completely taken aback when I was introduced to a fellow with twinkling eyes and deep-set wrinkles—not the kind you get from frowning, but the sort that happen when you smile a lot. I realized that while his passion for Sabbath-keeping had the capacity to incite lectures, his lifetime practice of Sabbath-keeping had softened him, sculpted his spirit the way water transforms jagged rocks into smooth stones.

Peterson writes that observing the Sabbath is not about what you do, it's about what you don't do. He writes, "Sabbath means quit. Stop. Take a break. Cool it. The word itself has nothing devout or holy in it. It's a word about time, denoting our nonuse of it, what we usually call wasting time." To keep Sabbath is to follow the pattern established by God in the Creation of all that is: a day of rest. It is a day to accomplish nothing in particular but pay attention to and celebrate the work of God.

My friend MaryAnn says that the trick isn't to tell yourself you're going to make time for Sabbath. Rather, this is what you say to yourself: "I am going to discover Sabbath time."

I think I get the distinction, and why it might be important. Surely, the last way I'm going to train myself to delight in the Sabbath is to write it on my never-ending to-do list. Buy milk, return overdue Dora the Explorer video to the library, honor the holy day of the Lord. It doesn't work like that. It just can't be turned into a task, because Sabbath is the opposite of a task. It is time that meanders, time that is free—or more precisely, time that bears witness to human freedom. People who are not free do not get to observe the Sabbath. And I don't just mean those who are enslaved in the traditional sense of the word, though certainly the theft of lazy Sunday afternoons is one of the many ugly indignities of indentured servitude.

Like most people, I manage to enslave myself to any number of Sabbath stealers. Busyness is the modern condition, and after Benjamin started working long hours, the flexibility and proximity of my job meant that most of the preschool drop-offs and pick-ups and a whole lot more of the housework fell in my column. I also learned quickly that while I might be less stressed in general as an associate pastor in a thriving parish, my to-do list is longer. Making time to do nothing means something doesn't get done. And sometimes . . . well, sometimes I think I just like to think I'm that important. There's a scene in Mad Men, that infuriating yet addictive television drama about 1960s advertising executives, where one of the smarmier characters smugly explains to his brother why he can't possibly take a vacation. "I'm very important to the agency—my absence is felt." Undoubtedly, this very same character is terribly paranoid that he is replaceable, hence his compulsive need to look busy, to verify his worth, to prove to himself if not the world that he is altogether indispensable.

The commandment to keep the Sabbath holy goes against this grain so radically it's no wonder our culture—even our Christian culture—has managed to sweep it under the proverbial rug. Out of sight, out of mind. If we do talk Sabbath, it's to recall the good old days of the Blue Laws with equal parts nostalgia and relief. It's charming that the stores used to close, but at the same time, I don't necessarily want to give up the option to stop at the market on a Sunday evening. I like my options; I like my freedom. And yet, there it is again, that word: freedom. It's a paradox. We are commanded to honor the Sabbath, yet honoring the Sabbath is the ultimate act of freedom. So why am I more likely to prefer the liberty to pursue our own affairs seven days a week than give up a little autonomy, sacrifice a little independence, to render that seventh day to God?

MaryAnn is the mother of three young children. She writes,

> Time-out in our house isn't a punishment, it's a little slice of Sabbath—and I use Sabbath not in the gauzy-pop-spirituality sense but in the stone-tablet commandment, "you have to stop now" sense. We don't always want to go into time-out. But we're better off having done so.

The five-year-old hears that "don't mess with me tone" in her mother's voice and skedaddles off to her room for her time-out. There is a common bankruptcy in contemporary Christian theology, and it's that we've decided we don't really want to take divine direction anymore. We don't want God to get bossy. We don't want to believe that God would cop that "don't mess with me" tone with us. We like the part of the story where Jesus forgives but are less inclined to meditate on the challenge to "go and sin no more." But when we filter out all the hard parts, we separate ourselves from the best parts. God may not always be nice, but God is always good.

This is why the psalmists wax poetic about loving the law of the Lord. They discerned a clear pattern: when they obeyed God's commandments, their lives were richer and more joyful. For all our perceptions of Sabbath as a dour, boring practice, in the Jewish tradition it is considered a sin to be sad on the Sabbath. Indeed, it is a mitzvah, or good deed, to have sex with one's spouse on the Sabbath. I really think God means it that we're to honor the Sabbath, but I also really think God means it that we're to honor the Sabbath by calling it a delight. By luxuriating in the life-giving, freeing gift of untethered time.

During our first August in Illinois, our family received an unexpected gift of Sabbath time—a weekend spent at Lake Michigan, not a full six weeks after I'd begun my new call. We almost didn't go; my senior colleague had to cop a "don't mess with me" voice when he encouraged me to take the time off, and this from a man whose leadership is anything but authoritarian. I didn't think I'd yet earned the right to take a Sunday off. But you can't earn Sabbath; once again, as ever, it is a gift we are commanded to receive. My supervisor had discerned how much we needed that time before we did. No sooner had we started making plans for our weekend than the stress of our cross-country move suddenly and finally began to dissolve. And so it was that on Sunday morning, while my new congregation gathered for worship, Benjamin and Juliette and I were at the state beach in Zion, Illinois. Although it was a gray and rainy dawn, we skipped stones, ran around in circles, built castles of rock and sand, and shared prayers of thanksgiving for all the ways God has abundantly blessed our family. (After which we headed to the Jelly Belly warehouse tour in southern Wisconsin, where Juliette ripped a thunderous fart during the video about Ronald Reagan's love for jelly beans. We laughed so hard I thought we were going to get kicked off the train. Ah, Sabbath with a young child.)

It was good to be at rest from my responsibilities at church. But without having spent most every other Sunday of my life among the communion of saints and sinners that is the church, I wouldn't know that our castles doubled as altars, just like the one Jacob built with a rock the morning after he wrestled with the angel. I wouldn't know that it wasn't enough for Benjamin and me to dunk ourselves in the brilliantly cold Lake Michigan just once; three times was so much more Trinitarian. I wouldn't know that the namesake of the sleepy little town of Zion is another word for the Promised Land. Yes, there is definitely something to be said for all those Sundays spent in church, tarrying with God among the people of God, rejoicing through song and word and sacrament. They invite me to enjoy the mysteries and majesties of Creation, and give me the language I need to pray and play more deeply.

Like our spiritual ancestors before us, we long to return to the Promised Land. In the meantime, we stake out a little Sabbath time on Saturday mornings, eating bagels in our pajamas and reading books until lunchtime. God said we must—praise ye the Lord!

19

The Beautiful Changes

I only have hazy recollections of life before Juliette. I remember the basic details and can picture myself moving through my days untethered to a small person. But what I cannot recall for the life of me is what it was actually like to *be* me. The moment I found out I was pregnant my brain was flooded with constant—borderline obsessive—thoughts about the developing fetus and the infinite ramifications of the developing fetus. Not five minutes passed without considering some aspect of having a baby. This didn't change after the birth of Juliette. I think about her all the time, and now that her sibling is fluttering around in my womb and gradually displacing my internal organs, I think about her, too. Neuroscience is a mystery to me, but surely this sudden and drastic reordering of my thoughts has reordered the very workings of my brain.

Sometimes I worry that all these thoughts of motherhood take up so much space in my head there isn't sufficient room for anything else. In the olden days, I spent an hour each day reading the newspaper. I was a relatively engaged citizen who more or less knew what was going on in the world. We finally discontinued our subscription; too many newspapers went straight into the recycling bin. It's not just that there isn't time to read. Though leisurely breakfasts are louder and rarer than before, I still read several dozen books every year. But the part of my brain that could process timely information has atrophied, squeezed out by the part of my brain that is constantly monitoring the floor for toddler tripping hazards and the air for the smell of poopy diapers.

When Juliette was eight months old, I brought her with me for a preaching workshop at the National Cathedral in Washington, DC. I had been to a similar workshop while I was pregnant and couldn't bear to miss out on another experience. My sister lived in Arlington, Virginia, at the time, so I devised a plan to bring Juliette along and commute to the Cathedral College from my sister's house. I even recruited my mother to come stay with us for the week so as not to strap Elizabeth with another infant, given that she had three small children of her own. The week was a bit of a bust. I felt a bit like a ten-year-old kid trying to commute to a residential summer camp; it just didn't work. I tried to refocus my attention and energy on where I was going during the brief drives between DC and Virginia, but I inevitably fretted about Juliette's disrupted nursing schedule while I was supposed to be listening to the exquisitely crafted sermons of my colleagues and wistfully considered all the extracurricular fun I was missing out on by dashing out the door after each session. That week we were each given a homework assignment: to memorize a biblical text we planned to preach. I never had much of a knack for scripture memorization to begin with, but I didn't foresee the train wreck that unfolded when it was my turn to stand before the crowd and rehearse my passage from 1 Corinthians. (That I had to follow a Baptist minister didn't help matters; I'm convinced those Baptists are born with the entire Good Book inscribed on the insides of their eyeballs. How else could she have recounted, word for word, a lengthy Old Testament passage without a single glitch? *And* make it entertaining?) I took my place, praying that the Holy Spirit would swoop in and sport me some hints. No such luck. I was the only workshop participant who utterly failed. I was certainly not the only mother there—all of us were members of The Young Clergy Women Project, and more than half had little ones at home. But I had brought my kid along. A great many things can be accomplished with divided attention; rote memorization isn't one of them.

***

Without a doubt, motherhood has changed me, and continues to change me every day. I feel a depth of love for my daughter that takes my breath away; it's so potent I don't even care that it reduces me to the language of clichés. I did not know that I could love another human being so completely and so well. I believe that. I believe I love my daughter well and that I am a wonderful mother. I believe the same of my partner. Benjamin is an exceptional father. The mere fact that I am able to claim our good parenting is another signpost of personal transformation. I used to be a profoundly self-critical person. No matter that I was surrounded by people who loved me, no matter that I was reasonably accomplished. I never thought I was good enough, and sometimes I convinced myself I was down-right bad. Now I cringe when I hear other women casually refer to themselves as "bad mothers," which isn't to say that I don't have days when I feel like a failure. Most of the time I look at this girl in my care, how delightful she's turning out to be, and marvel that I am one half of the parenting team that reproduced to create her. I can't even properly berate my physical appearance anymore. I half-heartedly bemoan the onset of wrinkles and the ever-softer concavity of my belly, but I'm so astounded by my body's ability to grow and feed human beings that I secretly love it. (The only thing more subversive than calling oneself a wonderful mother is admitting that one actu-ally loves one's body. Western culture is weird.) And then there's my face. I have never liked my face. For years I had terrible skin, and you never do grow out of a big forehead or a pointy chin. But I realized with a start sometime during Juliette's first week why she looked so very familiar to me: she looks just like me. And she is *gorgeous*. My math skills are second only to my neuroscience skills, but even I know that if A is gorgeous and A = B, B is gorgeous, too. Loving my daughter has helped me accomplish the countercultural, seemingly impossible feat of loving myself, imperfections and all.

Loving my daughter has also enlarged my capacity to love my husband. I instinctually respond to Juliette with a level of under-standing and forgiveness I've rarely summoned for Benjamin, and that understanding and forgiveness is bereft of the sort of resentful self-seeking that has often characterized my contributions to our relationship. I know now that I am capable of at least approximating the kind of biblical love we, like nine out of ten couples, selected for our wedding scripture:

> Love is patient; love is kind; love is not envious or boastful or
> arrogant or rude. It does not insist on its own way; it is not

irritable or resentful; it does not rejoice in wrongdoing, but rejoices in the truth. It bears all things, believes all things, hopes all things, endures all things. (1 Cor. 13:4–7)

Clearly, love for child and love for spouse are cut from different cloth. But I want to be as wholeheartedly committed to being a good wife as I am committed to being a good mother.

I can't breezily declare that I have a greater capacity to love beyond the small circle of my family. That isn't to say I don't love my parishioners; I subscribe to the philosophy that one of the minister's most sacred responsibilities is to love his or her people. But my priorities have shifted. Before Juliette, it was easy to let my duties at church poach time and energy that should have been spent on my spouse. I might have grumbled through those busy weeks during Lent, when evening Bible studies and worship services were tacked on to my regular schedule of choir rehearsals and administrative meetings, but I didn't erect any boundaries to protect my "family time." Nowadays I would pitch a fit if I had to be at church during bedtime more than twice a week. Family is primary. For this reason, some folks argue that single ministers—such as celibate priests—are superior to pastors who live and move and have their being within the chaos of a family. An unmarried and child-free minister can shoot out of bed when the phone rings at four in the morning and dash to the local hospital without first worrying if she will get home in time to get her kid ready for preschool or before her husband needs to leave for work. Some would even argue that the preferential love one has for one's family is itself a barrier to ministry. Jesus— himself a single celibate—taught, "Whoever comes to me and does not hate father and mother, wife and children, brothers and sisters, yes, and even life itself, cannot be my disciple" (Lk. 14:26). It's a hyperbole, an exaggeration designed to startle and challenge us into a deeper love of God. But *still*. I couldn't even begin to surrender my love for my family for the sake of my faith. By this standard, my spiritual life and my pastoral vocation will always be compromised.

But there is another standard, thank God. There is something to be said for life experience. I have, thanks to Benjamin's willingness to share his journey toward sobriety with me, a significantly greater understanding of the nature of addiction and recovery. I don't just enter a pastoral conversation about out-of-control drinking armed only with the book learning I vaguely remember from the unit on addiction in my pastoral care and counseling course. The same is true of marriage and marital strife. I've been there. That's not to say I hijack pastoral conversations with tales of my own matrimonial woes. I'm simply present in a different way, a deeper way.

So even if I have moderately compromised my pastoral vocation by strapping myself with a spouse and child, in noteworthy ways I'm a better pastor for it. Since Juliette's birth I've even developed an unexpected specialty: ministry with young mothers. For a good spell this newfound gift was untapped, on account of the demographics of South Bay Christian Church. But when a church member's daughter who lived overseas traveled home to give birth to her first child, I realized that my heart absolutely ached to offer her spiritual care through the process of becoming a mother. At her baby shower, I pulled her aside to make sure she knew that I really meant it that I would be happy to help in any way. She contacted me shortly after she was released from the hospital, strung out on the crazy-making hormones that wreak havoc on new mothers. We talked for hours while her beautiful daughter napped in the other room. I had so much compassion for her, so much understanding, and it showed. It was a gift to both of us; she received the support and care she needed, and I received a new sense of calling—though sadly, a calling that would summon me away from her mother's aging congregation.

My first project as the associate minister in a large church—a church teeming with young families—was to help establish a weekly discussion group for mothers of young children. I selected great material for us to discuss—Bonnie Miller-McLemore's book, *In the Midst of Chaos: Caring for Children as Spiritual Practice*—and hoped for the best. I estimated that we would have eight, maybe ten participants. Twenty-five women signed up. On the first day, while our children played down the hall under the supervision of church-funded, properly vetted childcare providers, we gathered in a circle and introduced ourselves. My ice-breaker question—*how has becoming a mother changed your spiritual life?*—turned out to be more of a tearjerker question. We passed a box of tissues around as each woman gave voice to the agonies and ecstasies of raising her children. Each answer was brave, honest, and unique, and it was fantastically apparent that we all—myself included—needed this sacred space. We needed a community marked by authenticity, respect, and grace, where the message is always *you're a great mother* even as we're inhaling wisdom from one another on how to become better mothers. I love that I participate in this group as a peer; I may scour the Internet for halfway decent Bible studies and send out the occasional gentle reminder about the importance of punctuality, but no one expects me to be a parenting guru. The greatest asset of the group is the group. Every night during supper, Benjamin and I talk about the best and worst moments of our day. Every Friday without fail, the highlight is that time with the moms; I can't imagine clearer evidence that I've found my true calling, that I am precisely where I should be, doing what I must.

And to think: once upon a time I wasn't entirely sure I was cut out to be a mother or a pastor.

Martin Copenhaver writes, "I do believe that, by donning such a role and by doing those things that are associated with such a role, being a pastor has made me better than I am." I concur, whole-heartedly. Being a pastor has made me better than I am. Marrying Benjamin—and *staying* married to Benjamin—has made me better than I am. And the little girl we named Juliette Louise has made me better than I am.

Thanks be to God.

Postscript

There isn't nearly enough Juliette in this book. There is far too much "me" and not enough Benjamin, but without a doubt, these pages are lacking in Juliette. The fact of the matter is this: it's hard to write about a baby. They don't say anything for a year, and spend another year speaking mostly in one- to four-word sentences. They are not, by literary standards, compelling characters. Which isn't to say I'm not utterly fascinated with my daughter; to this day, the almost imperceptible ridge that runs vertically along the cartilage of her nose is enough to make me swoon. It's just probably not enough to make even the most baby-loving reader swoon. Still, this is my last chance to present Juliette, who is, in my admittedly subjective opinion, altogether magnificent.

In no particular order, behold: *Juliette.*

She is a dancer. When she was about thirteen months old, we made up a song that consisted entirely of the lyric "Butt dance, do the butt dance," and whenever she sang it, she would start waving her big cloth diaper booty back and forth to the rhythm. Before long, she was busting genre-appropriate moves to various tunes; it was amazing to note that none of her Black Eyed Peas hip-hop choreography was duplicated in her Ben Kweller country routine. She recently began incorporating something in the neighborhood of pop locking into our regular Pershey family dance sessions; I think it is more likely that we have a future break-dancer than ballerina on our hands.

She is a healer. If I look or sound distressed, she says, "It's OK, Mama!" Without fail, it really *is* OK, and her simple encouragement is all I need to gain some perspective. Once, while packing a box in the kitchen in preparation for our California exodus, I banged my head, hard, against the metal corner of the oven hood. (This is a trick that could only be accomplished by a clumsy person packing a box; the laws of physics only allow for one alternate scenario:

actually *trying* to bang one's head, hard, against the metal corner of the oven hood.) I was already on edge, thanks to the impending cross-country move, so the moments that followed were not my best. I roared a garbled obscenity in the presence of my impressionable daughter and my clean-talking parents, and snapped at Benjamin when he attempted to comfort me. I stormed into the living room and flung myself on the couch to pout and clutch my throbbing forehead. Juliette followed me, pausing only to grab the foam egg she had been playing with earlier that day. She peeled my hand off my face and started to pat the sore spot, gently and purposefully, with her makeshift first aid tool.

She is a friend. I cannot stress this one enough. Juliette is social, outgoing, extroverted, gregarious, and convivial. Pretty much any synonym for "not shy" you can come up with. When she sees another kid, she turns to us and exclaims, "My friend! That's my friend!" She is also likely to boisterously inform her new friend, "You're my friend!" Not every child is copacetic with such an in-your-face approach to social networking. Sometimes we have to usher her away from a completely overwhelmed toddler.

On our way out of an ice cream shop last summer, we encountered three big kids—maybe six- or seven-year-olds—seated outside on the bench. She greeted them, and I quote: "Hi guys!"

But she matches her indiscriminate friendliness with a capacity for genuine friendship. Juliette met Lila when she was four months old, and until both of our families moved away from Los Angeles, they were inseparable. Lila gave Juliette a doll for her second birthday, right before she moved to Colorado. Juliette carried the doll around for weeks, cradling her so mournfully I could hardly bear it. She still remembers her first best friend a year later.

She is attached, yet independent. When we slipped through the back door of the attachment parenting subculture, I didn't give a whole lot of thought to the stated goal of attachment parenting: independence. The idea isn't to cosleep and breastfeed forever; it's to cultivate such a profound sense of security in the child that she is able to step into the world confidently—when she is ready. Juliette is still very attached to both of us. She is wonderfully affectionate, rolling over in her sleep to murmur, "I want to snuggle with you," and tucking her hand into its favorite resting space: just inside the cuffs of our shirtsleeves. But she is also wonderfully independent, exploring her world on as long a leash as we'll allow.

What else? She has huge emotions, but we're teaching her to take deep breaths. She loves books, edamame, and Dora the Explorer. She loves her family. To know her is to love her, and with very few exceptions to be known by her is to be loved by her. *She's just that great.*

Acknowledgments

This is far from a comprehensive testament of gratitude. So many friends, mentors, bloggers, children, preachers, artists, musicians, and poets have shaped who I am and how I write; I am abundantly blessed. *Thank you.*

Thank you to everyone at Chalice Press for giving me the opportunity to tell this story.

While I'm firmly convinced that it is God from whom all blessings flow, God sure does filter a lot of those blessings through three generous and prophetic organizations: The Fund for Theological Education, The Collegeville Institute, and The Young Clergy Women Project. Special thanks to Susan Olson; in convening The Young Clergy Women Project, she provided me with a social life, a collegial support network, and an avenue to write this book. Thanks also to Melissa Wiginton, Donald Ottenhoff, and Eugene Peterson for cultivating creative visions of pastoral ministry.

I am grateful to Steve Thorngate for opening the door for me to write for the *Christian Century* (a fine magazine every thinking Christian should read). I'm also grateful to Jason Byassee, Debbie Blue, Carol Howard Merritt, and Lillian Daniel for their support and encouragement.

Only a handful of these words were strung together in Kent, Ohio, but I treasure that place and its people—especially its writers, and most especially Maj Ragain and David Hassler.

Sari Fordham, Lee Hull Moses, Sarah Kinney-Gaventa, and Heather Godsey provided instrumental responses to first drafts.

On the second Wednesday of each month, I gather for a writing workshop with three of the most brilliant pastors and writers I know: Bromleigh McCleneghan, Erica Schemper, and Jenn Moland-Kovash. Their influence on my writing—and my sanity—is invaluable.

Lisa Hofmann is my former roommate, maid of honor, and Juliette's honorary aunt. She also has years of professional editing experience. You can only imagine how her intimate knowledge of my life and the English language enriched this book.

Lara Bolger doesn't just spot rainbows. She also spots typos and grammatical errors. I humbly repent from having written her off the first time we met.

The wonderful people of South Bay Christian Church taught me how to be a pastor and welcomed Juliette into this world with such love and fanfare that it still seems that she moves through the world wrapped in blessings. "We always give thanks to God for all of you and mention you in our prayers, constantly remembering before our God and Father your work of faith and labor of love and steadfastness of hope in our Lord Jesus Christ" (1 Thess. 1:2).

Thanks to the staff and members of the First Congregational Church of Western Springs for making a brand new place feel like home. Thanks also for the time and space to write—not every congregation would call a new associate minister with a massive writing project hanging over her head.

I am indebted to my family, a wonderfully witty, quirky, and creative bunch if there ever was one. I would be lost without my sisters, Elizabeth Dillow and Marie Taylor. Finally, thank you, thank you, thank you to my favorite and my best: Ben, Juliette, and the baby who was conceived, carried, and born while I was writing this book. Her name is Genevieve Laverne, and she has entranced us all.

Noted Works

Art

Bill Viola, *The Passions*, http://www.getty.edu/art/exhibitions/viola.

Books

Dietrich Bonhoeffer, *Letters and Papers from Prison* (New York: Touchstone, 1997).

Martin Copenhaver and Lillian Daniel, *This Odd and Wondrous Calling* (Grand Rapids, MI: Eerdmans, 2009).

Kelly Corrigan, *The Middle Place* (New York: Hyperion, 2008).

Anita Diamant, *The Red Tent* (New York: Picador, 1998).

Barbara Kingsolver, Camille Kingsolver, and Steven L. Hopp, *Animal, Vegetable, Miracle* (New York: Harper Perennial, 2008).

Eugene Peterson, *Working the Angles* (Grand Rapids, MI: Eerdmans, 1987).

Barbara Brown Taylor, *The Preaching Life* (Cambridge, MA: Cowley Publications, 1993).

Naomi Wolf, *Misconceptions* (New York: Anchor, 2003).

Magazine Article

John Ortberg, "Ruthlessly Eliminate Hurry," *Leadership Journal*, July 4, 2002.

Movie

Jason Reitman, dir. *Juno* (Fox Searchlight, 2007).

Podcast

Ira Glass, narr. "Unconditional Love," *This American Life*. Chicago Public Radio, September 15, 2006. MP3 file.

Poems

Wendell Berry, "How to Be a Poet."
Wendell Berry, "Manifesto: The Mad Farmer Liberation Front."

Websites

MaryAnn McKibben Dana, *The Blue Room blog*, http://thebluero omblog.org/.

Dr. William Sears, "Science Says Excessive Crying Could Be Harmful," AskDrSears.com, http://www.askdrsears.com/topics/fussy-baby/ science-says-excessive-crying-could-be-harmful.

CPSIA information can be obtained
at www.ICGtesting.com
Printed in the USA
LVHW03s1459290618
582300LV00011B/750/P

9 780827 200296